THE ART OF THE DANCE

O we can wait no longer,
We too take ship, O Soul,
Joyous we too launch out on trackless seas,
Fearless for unknown shores.

WHITMAN.

ISADORA DUNCAN AT THE PARTHENON

PHOTOGRAPH BY STEICHEN

THE ART OF THE DANCE

ISADORA DUNCAN

EDITED, WITH AN INTRODUCTION BY

SHELDON CHENEY

NEW YORK · THEATRE ARTS BOOKS

Library of Congress Catalog Card Number: 71-85671

Copyright 1928 by Helen Hackett, Inc.
Copyright Renewed 1956
Copyright © 1969 by Theatre Arts Books
All Rights Reserved. Except for brief passages
quoted in a newspaper, magazine, radio or television review,
no part of this book may be reprinted or reproduced
in any form or by any means, mechanical or electronic,
including photocopying and recording, or by any information or retrieval system,
without permission in writing from the Publishers.

Published by

THEATRE ARTS BOOKS
333 Sixth Avenue
New York, N. Y. 10014

Manufactured in the United States of America

THE ART OF THE DANCE

with reproductions of original drawings by

LEON BAKST, ANTOINE BOURDELLE,
JOSÉ CLARÁ, MAURICE DENIS,
GRANDJOUAN, AUGUST VON KAULBACH,
VAN DEERING PERRINE, AUGUSTE RODIN,
DUNOYER DE SEGONZAC AND
ABRAHAM WALKOWITZ

and with photographs by

ARNOLD GENTHE *and* EDWARD STEICHEN

PUBLISHER'S NOTE TO THE SECOND EDITION

AT A TIME when the dynamic energy and vivid life of Isadora Duncan are attracting new attention, it was thought valuable to make again available what she herself had to say about her art and the expression of life that was her dance, as published in this volume in 1928 by *Theatre Arts Monthly*. Undoubtedly the newer generations who could not see her dance must take on faith (or reject) that it was "divinity speaking, no less." But in these pages there is ample evidence that she could explain her art as few dancers have ever succeeded. Here one can readily be convinced that she was the bearer of a divine flame, and that she brought back to dance a religious element that had been lacking on Western stages for centuries. One can also see what a remarkable teacher she must have been, and how, although few continued to dance in precisely the same mode, the influence of her ideas expressed here, and of her spirit which shines through so much of what she wrote about her art, are alive today in the work of many modern dancers whose style seems superficially so far from that of Isadora.

The tributes of certain of her great admirers with which this post-humous volume begins were kept, along with the remarkable drawings and photographs of her by great artists of her period, as evidence of her art in action, but what she has to say herself, whether in finished essays, in drafts of letters to newspapers or to groups of pupils, or in program notes, is the important thing.

The publishers are grateful to the Akademia Raymond Duncan of Paris as the heir of Raymond and Isadora Duncan for permission to reissue this book.

PUBLISHER'S NOTE

THE essays by Isadora Duncan are here published in book form and copyrighted by express permission of the author's estate, by contract with Raymond Duncan. Rights of translation are reserved and are fully protected.

We extend our thanks for permission to reprint the following material: to Boni and Liveright for "I See America Dancing" (from "My Life"); to the Nation for "Isadora Duncan Is Dead" by Max Eastman; to the New Republic for "Isadora Duncan, Artist" by Shaemas O'Sheel; to the Public Ledger for an interview in "Fragments and Thoughts"; to Mary Fanton Roberts for "The Greek Theatre" and to Charles D. Coburn for "The Drama of the Future."

We desire to express our cordial appreciation to all the friends of Isadora Duncan who have helped to make this memorial complete and especially to the writers of the forewords and to the artists for their distinguished cooperation.

CONTENTS

INTRODUCTION *by Sheldon Cheney*   1

FOREWORDS

ISADORA'S LAST DANCE *by Raymond Duncan*   13

ISADORA *by Margherita Duncan*   16

ISADORA—MY FRIEND *by Mary Fanton Roberts*   24

ISADORA DUNCAN, ARTIST *by Shaemas O'Sheel*   31

ISADORA DUNCAN IS DEAD *by Max Eastman*   37

ISADORA—REMEMBERED *by Eva LeGallienne*   41

ISADORA DUNCAN *by Robert Edmond Jones*   44

THE ART OF THE DANCE

I SEE AMERICA DANCING   47

THE PHILOSOPHER'S STONE OF DANCING   51

THE DANCE OF THE FUTURE   54

THE PARTHENON   64

THE DANCER AND NATURE   66

WHAT DANCING SHOULD BE	71
A CHILD DANCING	74
MOVEMENT IS LIFE	77
BEAUTY AND EXERCISE	80
THE DANCE IN RELATION TO TRAGEDY	84
THE GREEK THEATRE	86
EDUCATION AND THE DANCE	88
TERPSICHORE	90
THE DANCE OF THE GREEKS	92
YOUTH AND THE DANCE	97
DEPTH	99
THE GREAT SOURCE	101
RICHARD WAGNER	105
A LETTER TO THE PUPILS	107
MOSCOW IMPRESSIONS	109
REFLECTIONS AFTER MOSCOW	116
DANCING IN RELATION TO RELIGION AND LOVE	121
FRAGMENTS AND THOUGHTS	128
L'Envoi	144
Editor's notes	145

ILLUSTRATIONS

ISADORA DUNCAN AT THE PARTHENON, *photograph by Steichen*
Frontispiece

PEN AND INK DRAWING *by A. Walkowitz*   4

PEN AND INK DRAWING *by A. Walkowitz*   5

DRAWING *by Leon Bakst*   16

ISADORA DUNCAN DANCING THE MARSEILLAISE,
   drawing by Antoine Bourdelle   17

DRAWING *by Antoine Bourdelle*   24

DRAWING *by Antoine Bourdelle, hitherto unpublished*   25

DESIGN FOR A BAS-RELIEF AFTER A DANCE BY ISADORA DUNCAN,
   drawing by Antoine Bourdelle   30

DRAWING *by Antoine Bourdelle*   31

DRAWING *by Antoine Bourdelle*   36

PAINTING *by Fritz August Von Kaulbach*   37

PHOTOGRAPH *by Arnold Genthe*   46

PHOTOGRAPH *by Arnold Genthe*   52

PHOTOGRAPH *by Arnold Genthe*   53

PHOTOGRAPH *by Arnold Genthe*   62

PHOTOGRAPH *by Arnold Genthe*	63
CRAYON DRAWING *by Van Deering Perrine*	72
DRAWING *by André Dunoyer De Segonzac*	73
ISADORA DUNCAN DANCING GLÜCK'S ORPHÉE, *chalk drawing by Grandjouan*	84
ISADORA DUNCAN DANCING A SCHUBERT MOMENT MUSICAL, *chalk drawing by Grandjouan*	85
DRAWING *by Grandjouan, suggested by Isadora Duncan dancing César Franck's Redemption*	96
DRAWING *by Auguste Rodin*	97
DRAWING *by Auguste Rodin*	104
DRAWING *by Auguste Rodin*	105
DRAWING *by Auguste Rodin*	116
SKETCHES OF ISADORA DUNCAN DANCING, *by Maurice Denis*	117
SKETCHES OF ISADORA DUNCAN DANCING, *by Maurice Denis*	122
DRAWING *by José Clará*	123
DRAWING *by José Clará*	130
DRAWING *by José Clará*	131
PHOTOGRAPH *by Steichen*	138
PHOTOGRAPH *by Steichen*	139
PHOTOGRAPH *by Steichen*	144

INTRODUCTION

THESE are the writings of Isadora Duncan on the dance. No one ever earned better the right to speak about this art, as she might wish, and without interruption. I am tempted, after collecting the essays that follow, to leave them without introduction or comment or explanation. All of us concerned want the book to be her own, to carry on her spirit, to quicken directly the work that is being done everywhere in response to her dancing, her courage, her teaching. But because Isadora Duncan is no longer with us, people are doubly curious about her writings: they ask, did she really compose all these essays herself, word for word? Is this all that she wrote about her art? Did she herself plan a book about the dance?

There are so many myths about Isadora Duncan, indeed, and so many questions, that some words of introduction seem imperative. Just as her dancing is, in the end, unexplainable, there are things about her writing that defy comment; but I will try, quite simply, to answer the queries that were put to me most often while I was arranging these papers for publication.

In the winter of 1926-27, when I worked with Isadora Duncan over the arrangement of some articles for *Theatre Arts Monthly,* we planned that *some day* the essays she had written about the dance would be collected, with additions, in a volume complementary to *My Life.* She was writing that extraordinary biography at the time, and was disturbed because those who were advising her kept saying, "Don't put into it too much about your art!" She expressed the wish, too, that there be collected for publication a selection of the portrait-drawings made by notable artists of Europe and America over a period of twenty years. The obvious answer was that an illustrated book about her art, as distinct from her life, should follow the biography. But she must finish *My Life* first. We arranged that I would see her in the following summer or autumn, to go over the material she would collect meantime. It was while I was on my way to Paris in September, hoping to meet her again, that word of her death came.

When a group of friends determined that the first memorial to her in America would be a volume of essays on her art, it was natural that its form should follow the general plan thus sketched by the dancer herself. This book is at once a memorial tribute and a completion of one of her own wishes. Lacking, unfortunately, that final shaping that she would have given it, it may be considered, nevertheless, far more than a random and unforeseen collecting of casual papers.

The present collection of the writings is as near complete, I believe, as is humanly possible to put together at this time. It includes all the widely published essays and program notes, many fugitive open letters and articles that had gone into obscure files, and a certain number of pieces apparently never before transcribed from the dancer's manuscripts. Inevitably the issuance of the book will call forth letters, memoranda to students, and possibly a forgotten manuscript or two in the hands of friends. But the collecting has been undertaken with the co-operation of the family, of Elizabeth, Augustin and Raymond Duncan, and of many of those friends who were closest to Isadora Duncan; and her own papers were turned over to the editor for perusal. Nothing that bears on her art has been omitted, nothing suppressed. There have been difficulties: there are four or five versions of some of the essays, due to the re-shaping of program notes for magazine use, or vice versa, or due to translation and re-translation; the handwritten scripts sometimes offer evidence of haste, and a word is obscure here and there. At moments of inspired composition, too, the sentences tumbled upon one another without punctuation, and the writer followed her own method of indicating emphasis and pause: the writing grew larger with the importance of a phrase, then dwindled, with dashes, mere space or a broadening of the pen stroke indicating full stops. It is a system expressive in the original, but impossible to transfer into rigid type.

Thus in editing the essays I have been obliged often to supply punctuation and occasionally to choose between words. But I have put one rule above all others: don't intrude unnecessarily—preserve the writer's own statement about her art as she put it down. Where several versions exist, I have tried to get back to the original, and this tracing back has led to the correction of numerous damaging errors and changes made by typists and editors. Occasionally it has seemed wisest to drop a paragraph from an article, where it was an exact or almost exact repetition of an earlier statement. Three or four pieces have been excluded as being outside the subject matter of this book: the art of the dance. These include an article on the art of Gordon Craig, which seems to exist only in German; one that was done only too frankly as a "promotion" article about Nice; variant statements of the plan for a school; fragments and lyric bits.

In fairness to the writer it must be noted that six of the essays in this collection are *translations*. Some of these were doubtless written in French, and translations are as much as we shall ever have; but in other cases there is evidence that the French versions were taken from English originals, since disappeared. In the translation from the original into French, and from the French back into English, there has been double opportunity for departure from the writer's exact shades of meaning. I have simply done my best in the matter. I have, of course, indicated in the notes which essays are thus translated.

Answering the third, and oftenest asked, of the questions, these essays are indeed Isadora Duncan's own. There are myths to the effect that her autobiography and her occasional magazine articles were undertaken in collaboration with "professional" writers. The manuscripts of book and essays are sufficient evidence to the contrary. There is truth in this: early in life she was influenced by and greatly indebted to the several members of her own family who were so close to her spiritually and as co-workers. During that period manuscripts were doubtless worked over jointly; and Raymond Duncan must be mentioned particularly in connection with the lecture-essay, *The Dance of the Future*. But that is the only reservation. Script after script exists in her own handwriting, characteristically, impetuously, put down. When the scripts had been copied out and punctuated, Isadora Duncan often corrected again, and added to, the typed copy.

For those who did not know the woman but only the dancer on the stage, it is as well to say definitely that we are not concerned here merely with a "star" who has risen, she knows not just how, to an eminence where her opinions are good newspaper copy. Despite the extraordinary directness of her art and her actions, her utter surrender to impulse, Isadora Duncan was master of the tools of the intellect. She based her philosophy on the value of the beautiful, and she trusted an inner emotion beyond any of the thought-out rules and systems of man: she was an "intellectual" last of all; and yet she was equipped with strength of will and mental capacity very unusual. Her heredity had meant contact with the arts and what is vaguely called "culture" from her earliest years: through her father who was scholar, collector, devotee to Greek civilization, and dilettante poet, and through her mother who was musician and lover of literature. Isadora spoke several languages, and occasionally she wrote in French. Her reading covered a wide range in philosophy, poetry, drama and history. She knew thoroughly and particularly Whitman, Shakespeare, Goethe, Haeckel, Rousseau, Schopenhauer and Nietzsche. She read widely for the pleas-

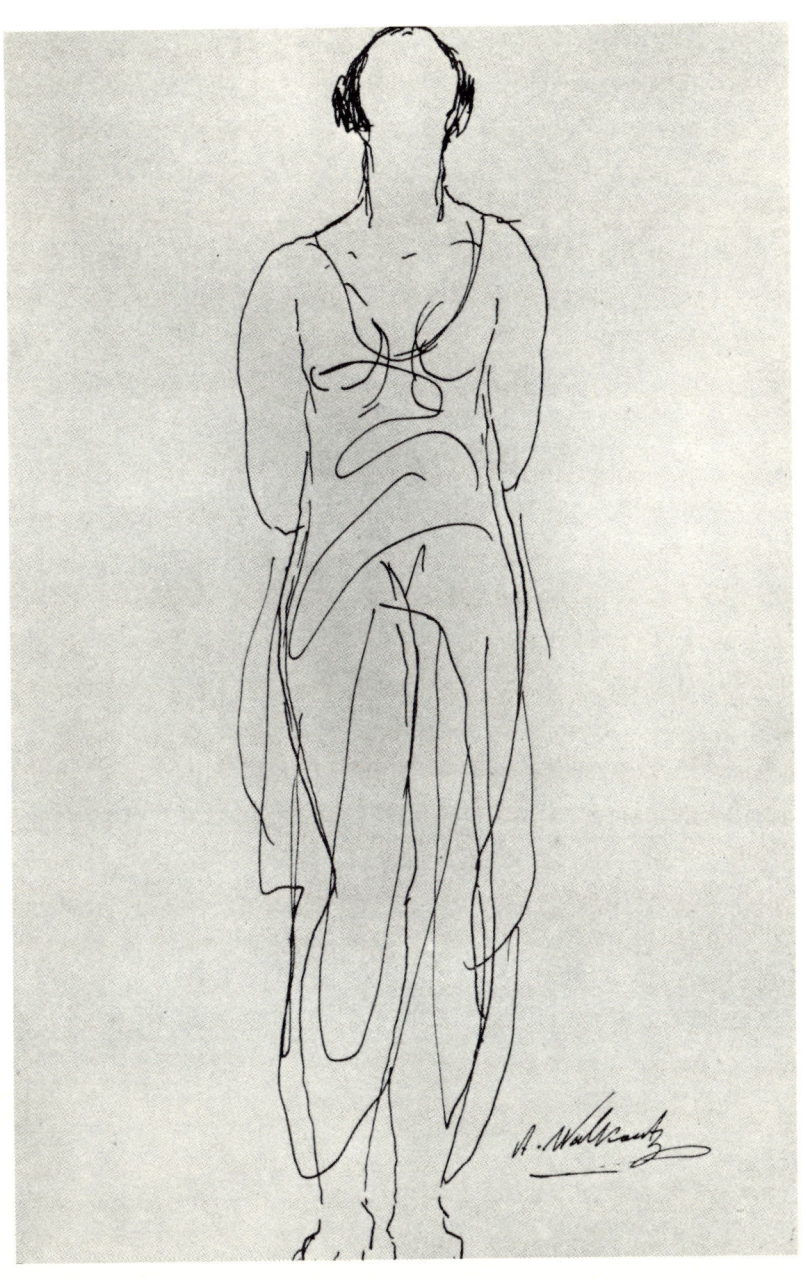

PEN AND INK DRAWING BY A. WALKOWITZ

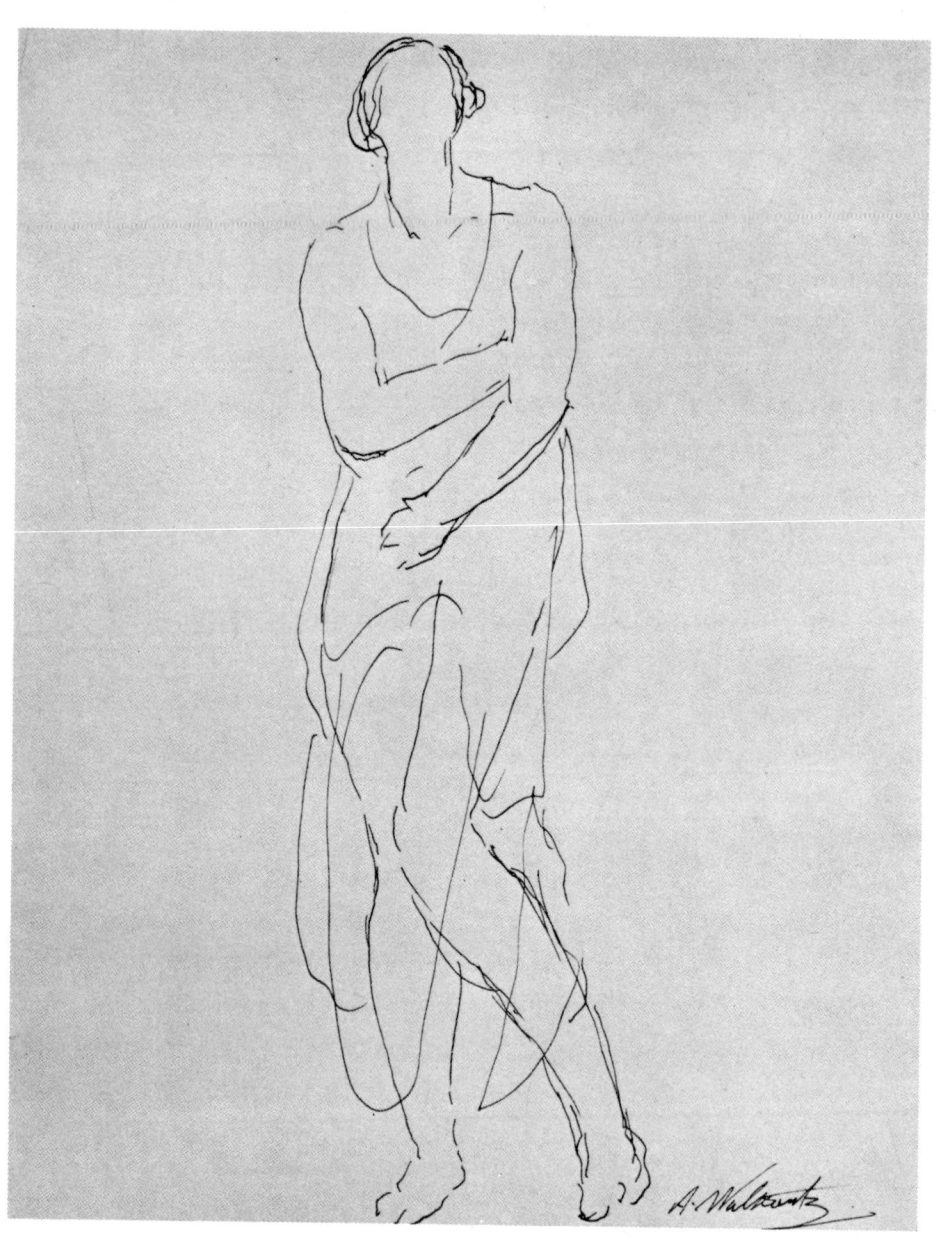

PEN AND INK DRAWING BY A. WALKOWITZ

ure of reading, but she also searched avidly through the literature of the dance, of music, of philosophy, for nurture of her art, for confirmation of her ideas. She spent literally years in museums and studios, with the art of the ancients and the art of the moderns. She was in personal contact, moreover, with many of the greatest creative figures of her time, with sculptors, painters, poets, actors, musicians. Probably no one knew more intimately the great men and women of the early Twentieth Century. I say so much because the newspaper reporters, in an age when flaming personality and outspokenness were fair game for journalistic "copy," left the impression, all too widely, that her intensity, her love of life and beauty, were not matched by mental gifts or ability in solid expression. She truly cared nothing for opinion outside those who loved her or who saw life as an expression of beauty, and she was willing to play a game with the journalists who catered to the rest of the world, to the conventional sensation-lovers. They did her injury—in the ordinary view—almost beyond repair. It is to be hoped that these considered writings—yes, strictly her own—will help to restore the truth about her.

No one pretends that these essays actually explain her own art. When she danced it was divinity speaking, no less. She comes as near to an explanation of the origin of her dance as any dancer ever has. She tells us again and again that the dance must come from within, from the soul, "from some melody of another world," from a divine fluidity. But when she danced it was a thing beyond explanations, beyond analysis, above words. And yet I think no other dancer can read this book without feeling new inspiration, understanding, new life, and certainly no dance-student will read it without profit, stimulus, deeper insight. But let us still make the reservation that nothing written can explain Isadora's own gift, the flame of beauty that burned in her, the way she swept across the world, and, by her dancing, shattered schools and traditions, accomplished a revolution, re-vivified an art.

No one ever lived her life and her art more indivisably. These essays about her art ought, indeed, to be read with the outlines of her life in mind. Without a glimpse of the living woman, the intense human being, the reader may lose much of the implication of Isadora sitting day after day, week after week, silent in the Parthenon, brooding over something to be discovered out of the Doric columns and the surrounding hills; or Isadora seriously asking a child, "Are all natural things beautiful, then?"; or Isadora saying to the massed proletariat children in Moscow, "Raise your arms slowly upwards and outwards toward the Heavens"; or Isadora answering, "Not only love but every part of life should be practised as an art." No one ever lived life more deeply, more directly, more magnificently. Friends, critics, casual readers, put down the book, *My Life,* with the same exclamation: "What a Life!" A few, realistic-minded or cynical, give the exclamation a sneering intonation. To the others it is a confession that this life is unexplainable, beyond words, in the directness of the woman's response to an inner urge, in obedience to a spirit, the divine in the human. Of all the people I have known in the world I think of Isadora Duncan as the one person whose soul was closest to the surface, least embarrassed by protective thinking or convention, whose very reaction was generous, creative, ultimately right.

To me there is an epic quality in her life. The picture of the girl-figure emerging out of Victorian times and customs, out there on the very edge of Western civilization, in California, vibrating to some wave of Whitmanesque affirmation, starting eastward with absolute self-confidence, conquering all of America and all of Europe for her idea, by a revelation, a presentation of her dance—in this picture of the march of the spirit of Isadora Duncan across the world, I find a greatness, a stirring elemental implication.

The reader of the present volume who has not yet read *My Life* will perhaps do well to keep that progression in mind—I have arranged the essays, after the first two, in approximate chronological order—and he may find it illuminating to recall certain "periods" of the dancer's life. First the Victorian beginnings, the girlhood, the dancing that was in a sense free already, but pretty, rather sentimental,—hardly more than a sweet child, in the frilled frocks of the period, but already burning with the desire to go forth and conquer the world for her "great idea"; and indeed in this period making her way from San Francisco to Chicago, to New York, to London, and so to Paris. Then the life of the maturing young woman, the love life lived fully, the dancing coming to a fuller expressiveness, with great successful tournées, lecturing in Germany, travels to Greece, motherhood, schools launched—success, indeed, homage, passionate love and tender love, and a world conquest well started, not for her own dancing but for the children of the world. Then a great and overwhelming personal tragedy, the drowning of her children; her life and her art almost shattered for the time; but finally a return to the dancing, less prettily, with a distaste for the sentimental things, a new note of depth, power, greatness. But while fighting the ghost of that sorrow, she finds it difficult to keep the schools functioning—the war does its part—and we read in successive essays her appeals for aid in establishing national or international schools, descriptions of the Moscow attempt, open letters asking that somehow she be enabled to pass on to the children of men all that she has discovered about movement as a means to grace in living. Her last essay contained the explaining line, "I have only made movements which seem beautiful to me."

The reader bringing some such background of understanding of the woman's life to the reading of the essays will find that they, in turn, complement and illuminate many incidents and motives of her living. Through it all one should remember the intense feminine nature beyond the artist-creator, the essential womanliness, the torrential but tender mother-love in her. I who have sought through her papers for these essays have continually come face to face with that emotional background of her art: her love of human beings and particularly her love of the child. The letter to the adopted girl-pupils near the end of this collection breathes it; the reports she exacted from the schools when she was on tour are full of echoes: routine matters ending with "Anna had a radish from her garden today," or "Irma has a new tooth." There are letters to her own children too—"Be careful about the stairs"—and then I have caught glimpses of the personal terror she felt, after they were gone, the confusion and the blank wall, when she who had so gloriously conquered life was perilously near to extinction by life.

These essays are naturally less impetuous than her autobiography—that biography that is above all, like her life, intense, revealing, direct, at times outrageous if judged by any accepted set of conventions. She made her own world, she wrote her own rules; she wrote her life in impetuous leaps forward, as she lived it. The essays are rather the crystallization of her thoughts between leaps. The connected story of her development as an artist is yet to be written—the material for it is well-nigh inexhaustible, and we may expect to see many a book that will attempt to present both the artist and the woman fully. But meantime this volume of her own writings may serve better than any other to fill the gap in *My Life,* out of which she left treatment of her art, on advice.

The tributes to Isadora Duncan are added, first as a proper memorial feature, and then with the hope that the writers, speaking of her dancing as seen from without, by her family, by friends, by critics, may serve toward a completer comprehension of her art. The picture can thus be made fuller, more detailed.

Nothing was more characteristic of Isadora Duncan's dancing than its disarming effect upon the artist-spectator. It demanded immediate surrender; all pre-conceived notions of what the dance should be dropped away. Creators like Rodin and critics like Lavedan and Faure forgot their cherished critical standards. That had been true, however, from the very start: before Isadora Duncan had gone farther east than Chicago, the greatest of Western sculptors of that time, Lorado Taft, wrote, "This rare artist is poetry personified. She is not the Tenth Muse but all the nine Muses in one—and painting and sculpture as well." Not quite so early perhaps, but from Chicago, came that essay by Floyd Dell with the line, "She has touched our lives with the magic of immemorial loveliness." In her foreword in this volume, Mrs. Roberts sufficiently quotes some of the leading New York artists of the day, Barnard, Henri, Bitter; and I may add that from letters and clippings the list might be extended to many of the most sensitive and creative men in the American art world: Edwin Arlington Robinson, John Drew, Jacob Adler, Percy Mackaye—and critics like Caffin and Meltzer. The London artists, during the next period, seem to have been more reserved about writing their impressions—one remembers Isadora's reference to their polite shyness, in *My Life*—but the programs of 1899 and 1900 remind one, in the list of patrons, of the lions of that era: here are Henry James and Holman Hunt, Andrew Lang and Walter Crane, Comyns Carr and Frederick Wedmore, all lending support of the "Dance Idyls of Isadora Duncan."

In Paris Rodin wrote, "Not talent but genius . . . It is art supreme and complete," and that explaining line, "She has achieved in sculpture feeling without effort." Carrière surrendered quite as completely; but it was always the sculptors who felt most akin to this dancer in her revelation of plastic form. Bourdelle confessed that he never would have done the *Théâtre Champs-Elysées* panels except for her. One might add almost endless names of widely known critics, writers, actors, artists, who were swept off their feet by the freshness of her dancing, over a period of ten years in Paris. With Rodin and Carrière on one program are linked no end of Princes and Princesses, Counts,

Duchesses, etc., and such really outstanding figures as Besnard and Clemenceau. Germany accorded her equally unreserved homage, particularly the artist group in Munich; and from Russia one may mention the printed tributes of Stanislavsky and Komisarshevsky.

I have considered whether this memorial volume should include a further selection from these many tributes. I have thus catalogued them to indicate the extraordinary range of creative people to whom the dancer appealed, and to suggest the uncritical response to her dancing. I have traced all this through hundreds of letters—and yes! in the files there are scores of poetic tributes: verses that range from the most pathetic inarticulate gropings of profoundly stirred souls to those lines by Percy Mackaye beginning,

> Through what vast wood,
> By what wild paths of beautiful surprise
> Hast thou returned to us,
> Diana, Diana of desire?

But after all, this is primarily the book of Isadora Duncan's own writings, and wants only an indication of that response, that quickening of perception, of enjoyment, wherever she went dancing.

The illustrations are tributes, perhaps, as much as the forewords. The artists have co-operated to fill out the essays with the most illuminating pictures of Isadora Duncan dancing. The thanks of the editor and the publishers go out to these artists. It may be added that four of them have announced the early publication of collections of their sketches or photographs of Isadora Duncan: Grandjouan, Bourdelle, Clara and Genthe. Fortunately, that so-valuable record of the spirit that was Isadora is to be adequately perpetuated. One may pause to wish that similar heed will be given to crystallizing and applying her ideas about education, about sensitizing the soul to beauty, about movement in the training of children.

While I have been working over the scripts this thought has come to me oftener than any other, this question: What is the world going to do with Isadora Duncan's ideas, with her plans, the spirit sown by her dancing and her teaching, her impetus? I have pondered over the sheer value lost to the world in the failure to heed her plea for a great international school of the dance, or of movement—for a hundred schools, everywhere. More than anything else, I hope that this book will serve to carry on her work, her "mission"—yes, she once called it that; that, outside the Memorial School now being started in Paris, and the school in Salzburg, women everywhere will increasingly realize the values still being lost out of child training; that educators will better understand the right place of beautiful movement as an element of full and harmonious living.

Isadora Duncan's personal influence has now flowed into the general stream of human living, and has turned the current, if ever so slightly. Her ideas, what she has written in this book, may yet be used further to turn the current toward those fields she glimpsed, where the freedom of the human soul and the beauty of the human body are twin actualities, not merely vague ideals—united in dancing. We who have had the gift of her own ecstatic and inimitable dancing shall indeed be showing ourselves unappreciative, if we fail to carry on the work, the plan and ideal, that Isadora has sketched in the following pages, in unaccustomed words.

Sheldon Cheney.

ISADORA'S LAST DANCE

BY RAYMOND DUNCAN

In face of the great dissension in the arts, during this last half century, in their strange separation one from the other, and their juxtaposition to the actions of life, like a genie directing the scattered orchestra Isadora appeared and raised her arms. She carried the Dance to celestial summits and sowed the dream of a new world.

Not a dancer was Isadora, but a prophet speaking the unique world language, voicing a beauty not only immense and sublime, but within the reach of and understood by the mass. Her art is the smile of the gods which at moments descends into our hearts, and her life is a reflection of the calvary of the world, in the mad crush of its misery.

Quite young, Isadora bloomed as an earthly garden sparkling in the sunlight. But bruised and wounded by the long years, her gesture created a radiant light leading the way to a superhuman ideal.

No one is capable of explaining her art and her message, but in the centuries coming she will be seen. The great movement produced by her in the world and in the arts of today is but the effervescence of the ardent kindling which will fix her message when the flame leaps forth.

Someone asked Isadora if there was a life after death, and she answered: "That is not my care; for what are we but sparks of a furnace, sparks dying in the eternal night, sparks of the primordial foundry, a torch of forms and figures, ghosts and shadows?"

We weep for her, but, enlightened through our tears, a great vision calms us. In the Théâtre du Châtelet, in the Trocadéro, great crowds were united; in New York, in Berlin, in the steppes of Siberia, in distant Afghanistan, in Athens and in Rome—everywhere an immense communion of the innumerable crowd, before the simple gesture of a woman. The vision of a divine art snatched from the firmament, and served as the Host to the crowd. The answer is there, and no critic can say, no artist can see, and no pupil can imitate. But the people have drunk and eaten.

In her last triumph in Paris, in July, 1927, rising in one sublime spring, she remade the life-road of anguish. Immense, and of a gigantic eloquence, she made come out from crushing death the pure flower of an eternal beauty.

We saw a promise, but we did not understand that the work was accomplished. We had hoped to be continually carried toward the heights of the unknown. The lesson is hard. For now it is for us to rise with our own wings and to accomplish, within the eternal torment of life, the sublime effort ever unfinished.

All these last days she prepared a new program: "Adieu, all my old dances," she said; "I will create one that will replace them; through Hell and its tortures I will pass, and to Paradise I will dance."

In her studio in Nice, during long nights, she danced the first steps of this great attempt. She put her arms around me and said: "Come, Dante, I, Virgil, I will guide Thee." And I followed, and I felt the beating of her heart and the rhythm of her breathing. I followed, my eyes half closed, for I dared not look; and together we passed through the horrors of Hell, which cannot be said nor seen, but which can be received.

One other evening, she called Jean Cocteau, who was with us: "Pôète, tu es Virgil, dirige mon frère Raymond vers le paradis où je serai Béatrice." He put his arm on my shoulder, and with his right hand, curiously thin and agitated, directed my vision toward Isadora dancing before us. And I opened my eyes wide, and it was not my sister that I saw, but a blinding celestial beauty. And I said: "This is a dance."

"Yes, but the music is lacking," she answered.

And today, all the birds of heaven have flown there high to sing the divine melody, the clouds cover the blinding sight, and my eyes are veiled.

And I wait long days, and perhaps even years, to join her and continue our voyage in the great and vast eternal night.

ISADORA

BY MARGHERITA DUNCAN

IT WOULD be easier, I should say, for a man to be a hero to his valet than for a woman to be a heroine to her sister-in-law; for this relationship is close enough to destroy illusion, while distant enough to be free from family prejudice. I can therefore speak of Isadora with some knowledge, yet with the impartiality of an outsider, since I entered the Duncan family long after my first impressions of Isadora Duncan the dancer had been formed.

Of a soul who has made such a contribution to the beauty of the world as Isadora, I would not also ask that she possess the ordinary domestic virtues. She might very well have left those to the women who have no other justification for their existence, and still have entered Heaven and sat on the right hand of God. If she had regarded me as an intruder and treated me accordingly, I would have said: "What of it? She is a great artist. She doesn't need to be anything more. If she does not permit me to love her as a sister, I shall still adore the artist and be grateful for the joy and exaltation she gives me from the distance of the stage."

But she was never anything but loving and kind to me, even considerate, sparing my feelings many times through the sympathetic understanding that is not often found in so positive a nature as hers. The lustre of her divinity was not dimmed by my approach to her within the family circle; it was enhanced by the glow of warm human love. She remained goddess and was perfect sister as well. If

From Svetloff's Contemporary Ballet

DRAWING BY LEON BAKST

© *Librairie de France*

ISADORA DUNCAN DANCING THE MARSEILLAISE

DRAWING BY ANTOINE BOURDELLE

she had faults, I could not speak of them, even if I would, for to me they are blotted out completely by her great lovingness. She had too much love in her nature ever to be unkind.

The first time I ever saw Isadora Duncan she was dancing on the Carnegie Hall stage to the music of Glück's *Iphigenia*. I experienced what I can only describe as an identification of myself with her. It seemed as if I were dancing up there myself. This was not an intellectual process, a critical perception that she was supremely right in every movement she made; just a sense that in watching her I found release for my own impulses of expression; the emotions aroused in me by the music saw themselves translated into visibility. Her response to the music was so true and inevitable, so free from personal eccentricity or caprice, her self-abandonment to the emotion implicit in the music so complete that although I had never seen nor imagined such dancing, I looked at it with a sort of delighted recognition.

I think this experience of mine must have been common among her audiences; for the desire for beauty lies at the bottom of every human heart and she gave it expression, so that in watching her we had a sense of satisfied longing. She so expressed the aspiration of the soul that no one could see her dance and be quite the same person afterward. I have known people whose whole course of life was changed by this awakening of their latent aspirations, who abruptly gave up what they were doing and turned to something entirely new.

This was not always dancing; but that reaction was a frequent one, and those who became dancers were right in their feeling, though wrong in their judgment. They thought it was easy to do what they saw her do, because it looked easy. Technique, I take it, is the mastery of one's medium of expression to the point at which the means disappears and only the result is seen; they mistook the perfection of Isadora's technique for lack of it, and thought that all they had to do was let themselves go, and the same beauty would come forth.

This very natural mistake led to much inexpert dancing, which made the judicious grieve; and none more than Isadora. For art was a religion with her, artists were the gods of her Olympus whom she worshipped wherever she met them, and half-baked or pretend ones were her particular aversion. She always maintained that art demanded the devotion of a lifetime, and to be a dancer worthy of the name of artist one should begin to train the body before the age of nine. That is why she taught only children, and never for money; because teaching was part of her life-work, a means of creating beauty and handing down her conception of the art of dancing, and could therefore never be bestowed lightly nor used as a way of earning her living. Of all the children who came to the first two schools she founded, that in Berlin in 1904 and that in Paris in 1914, the six girls known as "The Duncan Dancers" are the only ones who remained with her to maturity and can truly be called her pupils. Her third school is still carried on in Moscow by Irma, one of those six original pupils.

Isadora's uncompromising attitude on the subject of art often made her enemies, for she was ruthless in her absolute artistic integrity. I remember an incident at the *Masque of Caliban,* given in the Lewisohn stadium, New York City, in 1916. The author, Percy Mackaye, had persuaded Isadora to inaugurate it, and while waiting to begin, she found herself near a group of "Greek" dancers, trained by one of her imitators. One of these girls, excited by the occasion and the proximity of the great dancer, said to Isadora archly, "If it weren't for you, we wouldn't be doing this. Don't you feel proud?" Isadora looked at the poor child and said, "I regard what you do with perfect horror."

Of course the girl could not be expected to understand the grounds for this rebuff, and must have gone away much hurt. Later, in relating the occurrence to us, Isadora explained what she meant, putting her unerring finger on a fundamental and too frequent fault in dancing. "Their movements are all *down,*" she said, "grovelling on the earth.

They express nothing but the wisdom of the serpent, who crawls on his belly."

Isadora's dance was the antithesis of this. Her rhythmic line was always *up;* from her first joyous dances which seemed to float in pure sunshine, to those last tragic compositions which still expressed the indomitable reaching upward of the human spirit. This was the message which she was forever crying out to the world, from the beginning to the end of her life. To me it meant man's immortality, the divinity within him which lifts his soul toward Heaven when he is happy, and makes his feet leave the earth in the dance; and in the darkness of despair still turns his eyes heavenward seeking the light of hope and understanding. Whatever one's interpretation, it was always a message of courage and freedom, and all her gestures were free, open, outward and upward.

Early in her career, she conceived a dance typifying human experience which was like a mirror of her own subsequent life. It was not born of any piece of music, but of her own thoughts. She danced it sometimes, without music, and her audiences loved it and had named it *Death and the Maiden* after Schubert's song. In Paris the gallery never failed to shout for *La Jeune Fille et la Mort* at the end of a program, and once I saw her respond to that demand. We saw the gaiety of a youthful heart, suddenly stilled for a moment by a first apprehension of disaster —this fear thrown off and the gay business of life resumed—but the terror returning again and again until it overcame her, and she fell, defeated by forces stronger than herself. She called it *The Maiden and Life*. But I think her audiences were right; life baffled but never defeated her, till kindly Death snatched her away.

In her work, as in her life, tragedy loomed larger and larger, as outlined in this prophetic little dance; for the artist always gave what was in the woman's heart, and as that saddened, the change was reflected in her dancing. In the beginning, when her spirit was unclouded, her dances were the perfection of that joy which is symbolized by light feet that scarcely seem to touch the earth. As her experience of life deepened, new elements entered into her dancing. At first her program to the music of Glück's *Orpheus* had only the Happy Spirits of the Elysian Fields in it; later she added the tortured souls in Hades, and this first introduction of "ugliness" into her work was regarded by many of her admirers as the end of her career. They thought that no one would go to see her if she departed from the "purely beautiful."

Again, just before the tragedy which wrecked her happiness forever, another dance without music was born from her prophetic soul. She found herself doing over and over again, in her studio, a gesture that began in black despair, and ended in hope—eternal hope and aspiration. Thus, all unconsciously, she traced in art the line her life was to take thereafter; for she was so stricken by the sudden loss of her children that at first she was as if paralyzed; she not only could not dance, she had no impulse to express even her sorrow. D'Annunzio told her that her disaster was the most fortunate thing that could have happened to her as an artist, because of its effect on her work. But she would not believe him; for, as she said, grief clogs the spirit, numbs the soul; there is no impulse to self-expression in sorrow—only a desire to keep still and be let alone.

And so Isadora remained for a long time, all her usual outward-flowing currents turned inward to brooding inaction. Gradually, however, her powerful vitality asserted itself and she regained sufficient elasticity of spirit to feel the old impulse to express. She began to dance once more, but naturally not the old dances of joy. Instead she set to the *Poème Symphonique, La Redemption,* of César Franck that gesture she had been doing in her studio; and in it we saw not her private grief merely, but the suffering of all the world which was then in the throes of the last war. And because it was war-time, and she was filled with the spirit of fighting for liberty, she roused us with the *Marseillaise,* and with the *Marche Slav,* which seemed to bring an enslaved people finding freedom before our very eyes. The drama of the war was reflected too in the *Symphonie Pathétique* of Tchaikowsky, which was part of her 1916 program. It would have been impossible for her, in those years, to go on giving her old programs, as if nothing had happened to her or to the world. And yet there were critics in America, and no doubt elsewhere, who called these later programs a "substitution" for her earlier ones, because her gestures, appropriately, were larger, stronger and slower, and the enchanting lightness which had delighted the world was gone. These critics spoke as if she were a "performer," who, no longer able to do the old tricks, had learned new ones, easier ones. If they had stopped to realize that a long line is harder to draw than a short one, a long note harder to sing than a short one, and a slow movement harder to sustain than a quick one, they might have recognized that the change in Isadora's work was not substitution, but evolution. All great artists tend to simplify their means and intensify their expression at the same time. The movements Isadora executed were only a means to expression. If she moved less, it was because she was able to express more. I have heard people say of her last performance at the Mogador in Paris, shortly before her death, "Why, she scarcely moved!" meaning that she scarcely danced. But her public saw that she was more marvellous than ever before and had reached the pinnacle of her career.

One evening at Carnegie Hall, on her last visit to America, in 1922, she danced Schubert's Unfinished Symphony and *Ave Maria,* for the first half of her program. She was never more tremendous and universal. The cycle of life, with its eternal renewal, was before us. A gesture reaching toward the earth and then lifted upward recurred again and again, suggesting the love that nurtures children, that brings the whole race out of the bosom of earth up into the arms of God. And unutterable agony and suffering were there—but always that hopeful, loving, upward gesture.

I was so moved that I felt I must speak with her, and went to her dressing-room immediately, a thing I seldom did during the intermission. We wept together, both shaken by the experience we had just lived through. And she said, "Now I have finished. I have said all I have to say tonight. But because the manager insists upon variety, I must go on and do the Seventh Symphony, and I have no heart for it. I should stop now."

She was right. The rest of the program was only an indication of what she used to do, and it was a violation of her artistic conscience to reproduce an outgrown conception. It was the only time I ever saw her give less than a fresh creation of living emotion in a dance, for no matter how often she repeated a program, she always imagined it anew. Dancing was always an experience to her, not merely a performance, and never movement for its own sake.

In 1911 I was privileged to hear her enunciate this principle to her pupils in a way I shall never forget. She had been teaching them the dance of the Happy Spirits in her *Orpheus* program. After they had learned the gestures and the groupings, there came a day when that was not enough and she spoke to them something like this:

"Don't be merely graceful. Nobody is interested in a lot of graceful young girls. Unless your dancing springs from an inner emotion and expresses an idea, it will be meaningless and the audience will be bored. I'll show you the difference. First I will dance the music in the way I want you to dance it, then in the way I want you to avoid."

Whereupon she performed one of her marvels of apparent simplicity; a little skipping, a few upward and outward gestures of the head and arms, and heavenly beauty was created, the serene joy of the Blessed Spirits filled the studio. Then she executed the same movements, with no perceptible variation, but in such a merely graceful manner that I was astonished at the different result. I would not have believed that she could make a dance look like that. And she was not exaggerating her effect by any least simper of face or body. She was simply leaving out the animating spirit, and what was left, unbelievable as it may sound, was, as she said, entirely uninteresting. Except as an object lesson.

Remembering this distinguishing characteristic of her art—its meaning—we sometimes overlook the fact that she was, in the ordinary sense of the word, a remarkable dancer. There was nothing muscular or athletic about her, and yet she performed astonishing feats of strength, elasticity and endurance. No one has ever equalled her for lightness; not any one of her pupils—though they could all leap higher than she—and certainly no toe dancer, whose rigid foot removes the spring of the body at its source and defeats the very purpose for which the tiptoe position was obviously invented. When she danced the *Blue Danube,* her simple waltzing forward and back, like the oncoming and receding waves on the shore, had such an ecstasy of rhythm that audiences became frenzied with the contagion of it, and could not contain themselves, but rose from their seats, cheering, applauding, laughing and crying. Such a response could not have been evoked by any mere virtuosity. It was the spirit shining through that made her body seem lighter than air. The complete control of her mind over her body made her dancing a real marvel, both of physical mastery and of expressiveness. I believe that marvel never was before and never will be again. She was, in the true sense of the word, inspired; gathering within herself forces beyond the boundaries of her own or any personality, and sending them forth so that we all felt them, and were exalted by a vision of unknown worlds. We felt as if we had received the blessing of God, and looked upon her as one of His prophets, filled with the wine of His Spirit.

ISADORA—MY FRIEND

BY MARY FANTON ROBERTS

ISADORA was to me something at once magical and elemental, like dawn at the edge of the sea, pine trees in a quiet moonlight grove, or bells ringing from far, undefinable distances. And so I always find it hard to put her presence into words, even though my memories of her are crowded with her greatness and her loveliness, each significant, vital, a supreme justification of her all-too-brief, beautiful life. Yet, on the other hand, to write about her means an opportunity to express again my deep spiritual indebtedness to her. Isadora opened windows for the soul. I could never watch her dancing or listen as she talked without a sense of a quickened spirit, without seeing beauty more poignantly and feeling truth more profoundly.

Quite instinctively Isadora clarified life; so translucent was her spirit that the wisdom of the ages poured through her, and illuminated existence for herself and for those close to her. She ignored the superfluous; unconsciously, she eliminated all futility and pettiness about her. So far as I could judge, she never remembered an injury or held a grudge. She was too busy going about the great simple business of her life, the quest of beauty through her art.

Another fundamental quality of Isadora was her unworldliness. I have never known so unworldly a person. To be sure she was extravagant, as most unworldly people are. Money to her was something to be used or immediately given away either wisely or thoughtlessly. Yet she wanted money, asked for it, begged for it; there was no limit to

© *Librairie de France*

DRAWING BY ANTOINE BOURDELLE

© Librairie de France, courtesy La Revue de La Femme, Paris

DRAWING BY ANTOINE BOURDELLE, HITHERTO UNPUBLISHED

her desire for it. She wanted vast fortunes. But she wanted money all for one purpose—to build a great theatre for the dance—a theatre with the spacious beauty and democratic outlines of a Greek auditorium. She wanted to establish schools all over the country for little children, where they could be taught all the grace and charm they are entitled to—schools that would make children's bodies beautiful, strong, capable, that would make their spirits free and joyous. It stirs the imagination to think what the coming generation might have been if Isadora's schools had been established when she first began her campaign for the education of children through dancing. It was no small ideal —this international system of education, its goal to capture beauty for all people—an education no money could buy, each child selected because of peculiar fitness to the work, the price, devotion to the work, and each child given the full opportunity to develop, through music and movement, a perfection of body and an enlightened spirit. That Isadora should die without realizing this dream for human betterment is an almost unendurable tragedy to those who loved her!

Isadora's art was not only a sure and fine vehicle for beauty, but also a potent force to evoke in an audience a greater emotional sensitiveness to all art—toward all life, in fact. She seemed to create, as it were, audiences with a sensitized response to beauty, to rouse in people not only a greater love of art, but a greater understanding of humanity and always a more sympathetic appreciation of spiritual values.

Moreover, those who gathered about her, who assimilated her art, who loved her, seemed to gain a finer affection for one another. Wherever she lived she drew about her groups of people who were stauncher friends for knowing her; as well as great lovers of all art, of all fine effort, because of her art and her fine effort. In other words, she stimulated in people a vision that made them see beauty more unerringly and life more tenderly. The experience of people who came closely in contact with her life and who loved her, and sought her art, was, I have heard many say, like living through some splendid adventure hitherto undreamed of.

To enrich life for the world, that is indeed genius beyond appraisal. I increasingly understand what Rodin meant when he told me, one afternoon in Isadora's garden by the Seine, "that she was the greatest woman who ever lived." And, quite understandably, Rodin's sketches of Isadora were, I believe, among his greatest achievements.

It has always seemed to me that each thing Isadora attempted was supremely done—her dancing, her extraordinary production of the *Oedipus Rex* in New York, her training of little children to understand the arts, and to express their sense of beauty in dancing, and later her magnificent autobiography, a literary accomplishment, a spiritual achievement. She seemed spontaneously to create among those about her a generosity in human companionship. She made people feel the need and the power of it. She had a rare sympathy for all art and all artists. These qualities, as I recall, through twenty years of friendship, loom up before me as the expression of a splendid, liberated, powerful spirit, almost unconscious of self, but magnificently conscious of all that was divine in life.

As I think of Isadora's extraordinary power to express beauty through movement and gesture, I realize that I do not always associate this gift with the stage. I have seen her create fine sculpture forms through music without gesture; I have seen her do beautiful dances of arresting power without music; but also quite away from theatre and studio, I have seen her accomplish what was to me an even greater miracle, as she walked in flowing draperies through a green wood or on a gray sandy beach, or stood immobile on a rocky ledge as the ocean dashed spray up to her feet—always somehow, in quiet gesture or utter silence, seeming to reflect or gather within herself the splendor and majesty of immutable things.

I remember such an experience at Long Beach on a late fall day.

We were picnicking on the beach and I waited for her at the end of the boardwalk. In the early evening she came swiftly toward us. Back of her were the breakers rolling high in deep shining black waves, and the sky a dark sapphire blue. She wore an old, white, loose, woolen coat given her in Afghanistan by the shepherds. This caught the wind as she swung towards us in the twilight. She pulled a little cap from her head and waved a gesture of greeting, and as she walked against the tumult of the wind, her movements so free and gracious, she seemed like a great moment in one of her own dances. And the sea and the wind and the sky accepted her in a mysterious comradeship.

Perhaps one of Isadora's rarest gifts was as a messenger of beauty; many workers in all the arts felt this service and acknowledged it with deep sincerity. To Russia, Pavlowa told me, she brought "freedom in dancing." To Nijinsky she was "the great inspiration." I recall one memorable time when a little party of us were together at a studio luncheon in New York, and both Isadora and Nijinsky were there. After the table had been cleared away some one played the piano. I cannot recall who it was, but it was one of the great men playing divinely. And Isadora and Nijinsky danced together—Isadora creating the dance as the music flowed from the piano, and Nijinsky dancing with her as though he had rehearsed each entirely new measure for weeks. It was an amazing performance—Isadora's extraordinary power of instantaneous creation and Nijinsky's sensitive response to her mood and to the music.

George Grey Barnard once said to me, "Isadora Duncan holds within her genius an art to open untold dreams of man; no greater art has existed in any age, and none is more needed by our young world, where feet and life often drag heavy weight." Carl Bitter, who was one of her staunch admirers said, "the influence of Isadora Duncan's work is not confined to America; it affects the art expression of the entire civilized world." And Robert Henri, who had a profound friendship for Isadora, saw a quality in her work that made him think of "the great voice of Walt Whitman." "Back of her gesture," he said, "I see a deep philosophy of freedom. When she dances it is not only the beauty of her expression that fills me with emotion, but the promise she gives of a full and beautiful life for those who are to come."

Isadora was also a great teacher, for she *inspired* her pupils to a more sensitive understanding, just as she did her audiences. Years ago, when she had a temporary school in New York, she asked me to write my impression of it, which I did with much pride and humility, and which I quote here because Isadora herself liked what I had written:

"A great space, silent and high, separated from the world by curtains of blue; soft lights streaming down rose scarves; back in the shadows low couches in brilliant colors—this is the setting for Isadora Duncan's school in the heart of New York.

"A man (a musician, an artist) sitting at the piano. A Greek figure of ageless beauty, of ageless tragedy standing nearby.

"With the first chords of the music, lovely figures of youth appear, outlined against the blue, moving with gracious freedom; splendid white limbs gleam through gray-blue draperies; upturned faces are remote with ecstasy. As the music floods through these fluent forms, they are no longer separate dancers, but the spirit of youth bearing the world rich gifts of beauty; through these liberated bodies flow the melody of all the world, the joy of all the ages, bringing hope for the future of all races.

"Isadora Duncan 'teaches' her pupils by a gesture, a glance, a softly spoken word; and the response is magical. For she gives unsparingly from her own spirit of inspiration, courage, exaltation, and the message is received by free spirits in free bodies.

"Why should not the rapture which touches these children into ineffable beauty be the birthright of every child in every land?"

I used to go a great deal with Isadora to hear music and see plays and I always noticed the way in which she gave her whole-hearted attention to whatever was being presented. If some one in her studio played for her, or sang, or read poetry, her delight and interest were intense and genuine; in fact, she had a rare courtesy toward all life and all people. There were no barriers to her respect for humanity. Naturally she loved best what gave her greatest joy—the poet, the sculptor, the painter, the writer; but for all people, if they came to her to show their achievement or to ask for help, she had an instant response, a soul that never failed to give sympathy and understanding.

For her art, Isadora drank from the deep springs of life, and these springs she found in amazing places, for during her life she walked wherever she chose; there were no closed doors to her interest and love. The pathways of her life were sometimes rocky and sometimes rose-strewn, but she moved over them with enchanted feet, with shining eyes, with an outlook that touched the horizon. There was an ineffable quality to her spirit that kept people from mourning over her, and that kept her, too, from surrendering to the shadows of life. She moved from tragedy to tragedy as though she were on mountain peaks, and at the very end of her life she danced as though her art were her sole preoccupation, as though expressing beauty was the single reason of her existence.

Isadora's own ideal of what the future might bring for the world she once wrote for a program I did for a New York performance, as follows: "Oh, she is coming, the dancer of the future; the free spirit, who will inhabit the body of new women; more glorious than any woman that has yet been; more beautiful than the Egyptian, than the Greek, the Early Italian, than all women of past centuries—the highest intelligence in the freest body!"

And for the same program she asked me to quote something of Walt Whitman which she said had been a lasting inspiration to her and influence in her life: "O we can wait no longer. . . . We too take ship, O soul. . . . Joyous we too launch out on trackless seas, fearless for unknown shores. . . ."

To those who have seen Isadora dance, and most of all to those of us who loved her, her death is an irreparable loss as her life was a transcendant gift.

© *Librairie de France*

DESIGN FOR A BAS-RELIEF AFTER A DANCE BY ISADORA DUNCAN

DRAWING BY ANTOINE BOURDELLE

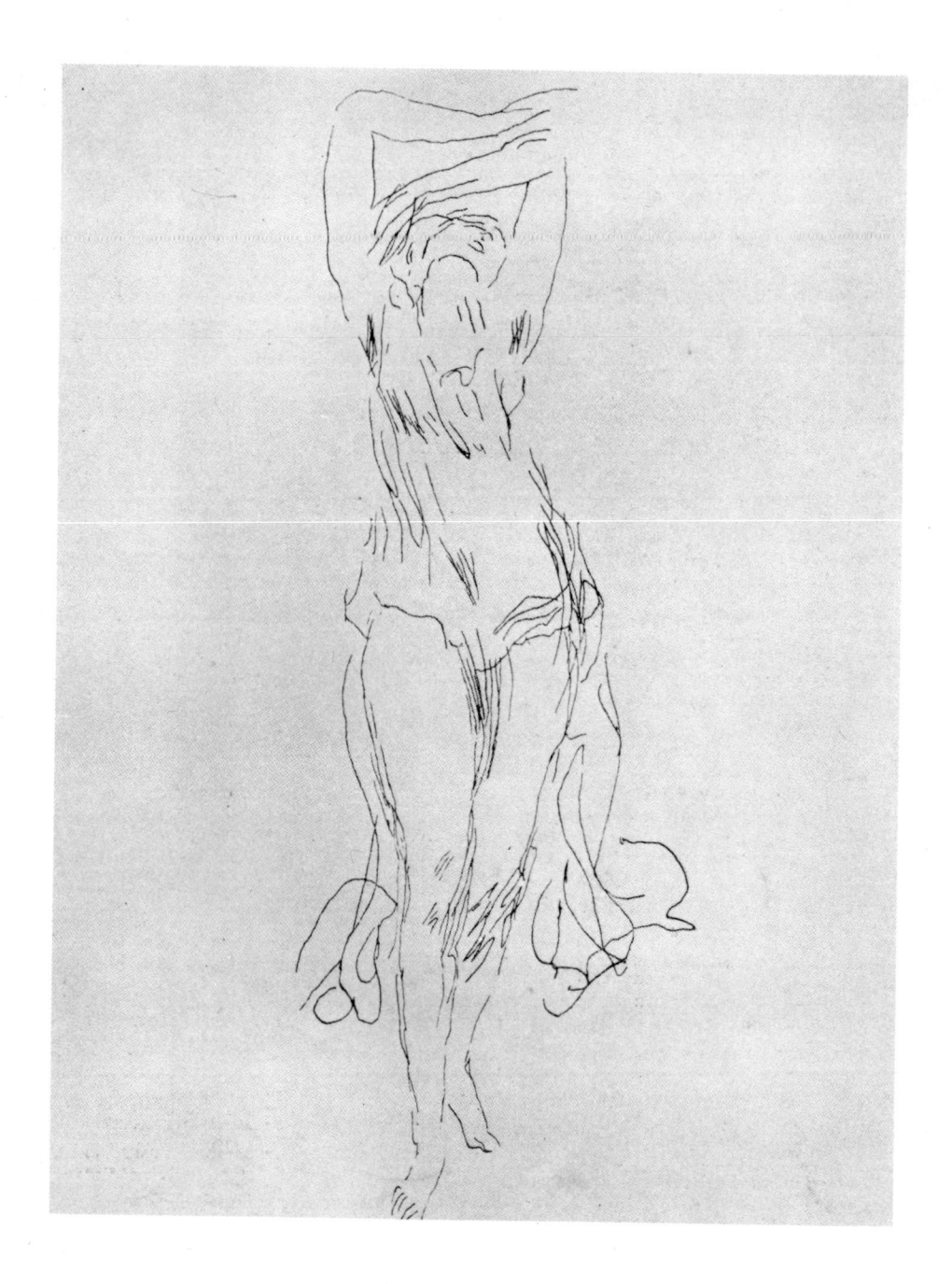

DRAWING BY ANTOINE BOURDELLE

ISADORA DUNCAN, ARTIST

BY SHAEMAS O'SHEEL

Europe will mourn her with a sharper grief and a more poignant realization of the void that is left by her going. French and Germans, Russians and Italians, all are Good Europeans in reverence for genius. To them Isadora was one with the glory that was Greece, one with the glory of all great art in all ages, peer of Phidias and Botticelli and Michelangelo, sister of great Ludwig, and Glück, and Chopin, and Wagner; but our awareness of her as an artist was clouded by our interest in her as good copy for sensational stories in the public prints. Yet in the shadow of the fantastic tragedy at Nice, it is we most of all who should mourn and remember and honor our own. For she was our own, and it seems to me that no woman born of centuried Europe could have done what she did—that somehow it was destined and appropriate that America should cradle the woman who recreated in our day the oldest of the arts.

Whether there is a kind of Platonic absolute of art is a question in dispute since the days of Lessing; but if the revelation of beauty and the sanction of wonder, the awaking of aspiration and the disquieting of thought and the release of energy for purposes beyond food and shelter, raiment and safety, are the ends for which all the arts alike assault the mind and soul by the several portals of the senses, it seems to me that Isadora Duncan was the greatest artist of our times; for it seems to me that more than any other in the first quarter of this century, she brought us, fused and incandescent, that awakening and disquieting and release. It is necessary to say this to the generations who never can see her and who cannot be aware to what extent all the art they touch will bear her hidden impress; for every poet and musician and plastic artist of her generation sat at her feet, and she entered into sculpture and painting, music and poetry so pervasively, so organically, that her influence can be traced no more precisely than the rain that falls in the forest can be traced to the arbutus and the oak-leaf that it nourishes. Alas that her art, the most robust in facing the moment, was the most fragile in the fingers of Time!—the price of its incomparable aliveness was its utter evanescence. Words must do their poor best to preserve some memory of a thing that was as instant and perfect and beyond the power of words as the slant of an April shower in sunlight over green hills, or the toss of a branch of young leaves, or the arched flight of a marten, or the breaking of white waves on dark waters. Words!—why did not some of the pompous promoters of the new "art" of the motion pictures ever think of devoting a trifling sum to making a record of Isadora's dancing? Why did she never think of it herself? At least some pale and imperfect image of her might have gone down to the generations to make evident what I and others abler than I must despair of telling with words.

When Isadora went to Munich, the dance as a great art did not exist. There was the lace-and-china-and-powder-puff prettiness of the ballet, and there was dramatic dancing, leaning heavily on décor and properties and costumes, and striving to act out a story that it was fundamentally a bit ridiculous to act out in a dance. But the dance as a great art, holding up its head among the hierarchies with the art of Palestrina and Beethoven and Wagner, with the art of the sculptor of the Sphinx and the painter of bisons in the cave of Altimira, with Leonardo and Rembrandt and Rubens, Greco and Monticelli and Van Gogh, with Homer, Chaucer, Coleridge, Shelley, Yeats—as such an art the dance did not exist. She re-created it from the same pregnant elements whose fiery substance has been seized by all great artists: nature, wonder, the ancient mysteries and the old symbols—seen with high intelligence, felt with a sensitiveness aware of overtones and undertones, moulded by genius, the shaping power that is not to be measured nor understood.

Words are of little use to describe any good dancing, and of how little, therefore, to suggest hers! There was a bare stage, flooded with equable light, and a background of unfigured curtains whose heavy folds reached up into darkness. Bare of limb and splendid of limb she came and moved before us; like a curled leaf drifting over the grass. Plutarch wrote that music is audible dance and the dance is silent music. Say rather visible music, music translated for another sense, doubly alive. She danced only to great music: Beethoven—the Fifth and the Seventh Symphonies—and Chopin, and Glück in whose ineffable melodies passion and hope and despair are intensified to serenity; and such music she made visible with "majestic instancy."

Here were grace and sheer visual beauty in pulse-quickening loveliness; but it was not these that so moved us. There was something else. It was that Isadora's art was great *symbolic* art. Her stage was the wind-drifted border between flowering meadow and sandy beach on the margin of some nameless sea where the horn of Poseidon faintly echoes, and Kypris, the World's Desire, might be born of any wandering wave. The folded curtain became the ancient trees that guard the vaporous cleft of the Pythoness in the forests of Delphi, and the towering crags of the Caucasus, at the end of the world, where Prometheus knows the vulture and remembers the love of man and the vengeance of gods. And she was the soul of man confronting nature and the enigma of life, brave and troubled and terrified among the mysteries. This was not drama. Others have given us dramatic dancing, and at times during her later years, Isadora herself, in her endless experimenting, declined into dramatic dancing. But I write of her art at its greatest—and no artist ever kept to the very peak of achievement with more sustained mastery. Dramatic art—in dance or play, music, painting, sculpture or poetry—attempts to wring emotional or intellectual effects from the actual; builds from the surface; its gestures, at best, dignify the obvious. Symbolic art goes back through Time even to beginnings that are forgotten; evades the ephemeral and twines like a tendril about the essential, drawing sustenance from all great moments; penetrates below surfaces, through flesh and nerves to the quick core of being; taps the very sources of joy and grief, and startles from their slumber those race-memories that live unnoted in the still places of the soul. Let the wise of future generations understand that more than any other of this age, Isadora was the naïve companion and messenger of the stars and the sword, the rose and the rood, mystery, and wonder, and eternity.

That was why people wept when they watched her. People came out of the brisk stream of life flowing up Broadway, and sat in the Metropolitan Opera House or Carnegie Hall, a few feet away from the hard surfaces and pert hopes and immediate worries of that stream, and she tuned them like lutes and swept them with rhythms their forbears had forgotten ages ago, and the beauty and wonder of it summoned tears as the rod of Moses wrung water from the rock. It was an emotion as far removed from sentimentality as her art was distant from prettiness. Any natural man, normally concerned with daily labor and material affairs—truck-driver, lawyer, bank president—who might have come into her presence, would, after a brief orientation, have felt the power of her subtle and imperious magic, would have experienced understanding and refreshment and release.

It was customary to refer to Isadora's dancing as "Greek." But she herself wrote that she went to nature as primitive man had done. She wrote that the dance was the earliest of the arts, and that primitive man had been inspired directly and immediately by the movements of wind and wave and bird and beast. She found image and evidence of this in

Greek sculpture and frescoes and the figures on vases. Rationalistically she overlooked, but instinctively she understood, that many of these were made in a time of sophisticated and urban civilization, and pictured a dance that was not immediately from nature, but was part of centuried ritual. But there are works of Greek art that are immediately from nature as the wave is from the sea. Such are many archaic figures, and such are the Wingless Victory and the Victory of Samothrace. It is of these that she was sister. Raymond Duncan re-created with more uncanny exactitude the measured, angular, clearly ritualistic gestures of Greek dancing. He went to the vases and reliefs; but Isadora went to Niké Anapteros, to Nature; Greece was merely on the way. It is not surprising to those who sensed how utterly from within her great art came, that she traces the roots of it to her Irish and Scots blood, to that American pioneering impulse which made her family a part of the great covered-wagon trek across the prairies, to the majesty of the Rockies and the spell of the Pacific, and to the great winged chants of Walt Whitman.

When I first wrote about Isadora I predicted, as others did and as she did, that the dance as a great art participated in by multitudes, was about to be re-established in the world. The heavy hand of disillusionment long since bruised the flower of that enthusiasm. Yet I think we can see and say now that the seed of her hope has living roots. Certainly the art of the dance is in very different state now, and directly because of her, than before she came. Her example liberated the Russian ballet and gave it creative power. Some of her own pupils are artists whose stature suffers only in comparison with her. Fundamentally today dancing is understood to be not a thing of mincing toes, but an aesthetic exercise of the whole body; and that is a vindication of her courageous intelligence. Bare-legged females cavorting on the lawns of women's colleges and finishing-schools clad in "two yards of cheesecloth for self-expression" are at times very trying, and from the hundreds of "classical dancing schools" that now dot the land little may come forth, yet this is better than the ballet tradition which cramped the mind and spirit while it tortured the body; and it is well that soil is kept fallow for the seed of genius that has its way of taking root suddenly and always unpredictably. For it is individual genius that matters. Lesser artists cloud the glory of the great. For the making of an Isadora there is needed intelligence of the highest order. She had it. There is needed a vital and brooding understanding of nature and life. She had it. There is needed that autochthonous spark called genius. She had it—more than any woman artist since Sappho.

DRAWING BY ANTOINE BOURDELLE

From the Munich Jugend

PAINTING BY FRITZ AUGUST VON KAULBACH

ISADORA DUNCAN IS DEAD

BY MAX EASTMAN

ISADORA DUNCAN was the last friend I saw when I left Europe this spring. She stood in the little crowd on the platform at the Gare Saint Lazare. I was standing at the car window, laughing and half crying at the sadly funny excitement of people parting with their friends, and suddenly I heard her voice calling my name and "Goodbye!" She raised her hand when I caught sight of her, and stood still with it raised in the air and moving slowly in a serene and strong benediction. A great beam of that energetic and perfectly idealistic light shone out of her eyes to me. She looked very great. She looked like a statue of real liberty.

It made me sad for a long time, because greatness in this little world is sad. Greatness coming to an unhappy end is almost unendurable, and I had felt that Isadora was coming to an unhappy end. I felt it underneath all the delightful bubbling of her mirth when I saw her during the winter in Cannes. It was at the house of our friend, Lucien Monod, a Communist and an artist. She had just received a cablegram that money would be forwarded for her memoirs, and she was full of laughing joy—that wild, reckless, witty joy that all her friends remember. Isadora could sprinkle the whole world with her wit and make it shine. A lot of stupid Americans—indeed almost all of stupid America—imagine that they laughed at Isadora. They are completely mistaken. Isadora laughed at them. She laughed as Rabelais would laugh at them, or Montaigne, or Shakespeare, or Aristophanes. Any great man or woman would laugh at them. And Isadora Duncan was one of the great men and women—more indubitably so, I think, than any other artist who has lived in our time. They speak of Duse and Sarah Bernhardt and Isadora as a trio of great women, but Isadora was incomparably above the other two. She was not only a supreme artist as they were—endowed by nature with momentous power and the perfect gift of restraining it—but she was also a mind and a moral force. She used her momentous power, as the giants of mankind have always done, not only to entertain the world but to move it.

And she did move it. It is needless to tell how she changed the art of dancing in our time. She was a revolution in that art, and so to some extent in the whole art of the theatre. All the civilized world acclaimed her, and recognized in that young brave girl's beautiful body, running barefoot and half-naked, running and bending and pausing and floating in a stream of music, as though the music had formed out of its own passion a visible spirit to live for a moment and die when it died—all the world recognized in that an artistic revolution, an apparition of creative genius, and not merely an achievement in the established art of the dance.

But I think few people realized how far beyond the realm of art —how far out and how deep into the moral and social life of our times the influence of Isadora Duncan's dancing extended. All the bare-legged girls, and the poised and natural girls with strong muscles and strong free steps wherever they go—the girls that redeem America and make it worth while to have founded a new world, no matter how badly it was done—they all owe more to Isadora Duncan than to any other person. And the boys, too, that have a chance to be unafraid of beauty, to be unafraid of the natural life and free aspiration of an intelligent animal walking on the earth—all who have in any measure escaped from the rigidity and ritual of our national religion of negation, all of them owe an immeasurable debt to Isadora Duncan's dancing. She did not only go back into the past to Athens to find that voluntary restraint in freedom that made her dancing an event in the history of art. She went forward into the future—farther, I suppose, than Athens—to a time when man shall be cured altogether of civilization, and return, with immunity to that disease if with few other blessings, to his natural home outdoors on the green surface of the earth. That made her dancing an event in the history of life.

Isadora was exiled—banished by more than an accident of the marriage law—from America. It was inevitable that she should be. America had never seen a woman genius before, and could not think of anything else to do with her. But nevertheless Isadora was very American. The big way in which she conceived things, and undertook them, and the way she succeeded with them, was American. Even her faults were American—her passion for "pulling off stunts" —"gestures" is the way she would say it—was American. She made a grand sport of her public position and character. She played with publicity like a humorous Barnum. Even her extravagant and really bad irresponsibility, which went almost to the point of madness in late years, was in the reverse sense an American trait. It was an exaggerated reaction against America's "righteousness." *Wrongtiousness* is what you would have to call it if you wished to appraise it with a sense of its origin.

America fighting the battle against Americanism—that was Isadora. From that battle incomparable things are to come—things that will startle and teach the world. And Isadora led the way into the fight all alone, with her naked and strong body and her bold character, vivid as an Amazon. If America triumphs over itself—over its cheap greed and prudery, its intellectual and moral cowardice, its prudent and prurient hypocrisy—if America triumphs over that, Isadora Duncan will be sculptured in bronze at the gate of the Temple of Man in the new day that will dawn. She will stand there, poised in terrible impatience, knee raised and arms tensely extended as in the *Marche Militaire* or the Scythian warrior's dance—beautiful—a militant and mighty woman, the symbol and the veritable leader of those who put on their courage like armor and fought for the affirmation of life in America.

ISADORA REMEMBERED

BY EVA LE GALLIENNE

Rather than dwell upon Isadora Duncan as a human-being, the most vibrantly *alive* of human-beings, imbued with the vitality of the earth itself, generous, big, noble and pure with the nobility and purity of great and simple things, I prefer to recall some of her thoughts and ideals concerning the relation of her art with Life, with growth, with the culture of the race.

Finding it impossible to think of Isadora as dead, I shall try and imagine that tomorrow I shall hear her talk of all these things, so immeasurably dear to her, so integrally a part of her; that I shall see her face light up and hear her voice, always even in the gravest moments of her thought so full of an elfin humor.

Her greatest wish was to bring the dance close to the *lives* of the people. The dance was not merely an art to her, but was part of her very being; she was *obliged* to dance, as we are obliged to breathe. There was to her no difference between dancing and living. She felt that through the dance one became inseparably a part of the great rhythm of the Universe, and that this harmony between Self and the Centre of Being resulted as a matter of course in harmonious living.

Her ideas on education were not so much radical and revolutionary as they were reactionary in the sense of travelling back over the years to the ancient Greeks, to the time when physical, mental and spiritual culture formed a balanced whole. She had a wonderfully clear vision of the *rightness* of this. She believed that through rhythm a child could be given an understanding of beauty, of a poem, a philosophy or a mathematical equation; that from a beautiful body perfectly poised would spring a beautiful mind and spirit in absolute co-ordination. This was surely the ancient ideal. We have travelled far from it, and the arrogance of our modern civilization has made us narrow and fearful of anything that seems to upset our well-ordered scheme of things. This is perhaps the reason why no country would allow Isadora Duncan a free rein for experiment.

Communist Russia was the only country that even for a moment entered into her thought and did not quite turn a deaf ear.

One of my most thrilling memories is hearing Isadora tell of the thousand children whom she had trained, dancing through the streets of Moscow. She often said it was the happiest moment of her life; but she would have set all the children of the world dancing, and through this dance of natural rhythm have given them freedom of body and of mind.

She felt so strongly the cruelty and stupidity of chaining a little child to an ink-stained desk, in a stuffy room, confronted by thousands of words, devoid of all meaning by the time they had been hammered into that rebellious little head.

Isadora was above everything American. Her thoughts continually turned toward this country that she loved above all others. But she could not love blindly, and America is perhaps still too young to endure criticism. Isadora saw the infinite possibilities, the wide horizons, the pulsing vitality, the strength, the joy of this country, and longed to throw her vision and her wisdom at its feet. How strange it is that a country born and cradled in Revolution should so consistently turn its austere back on its greatest and most typical children. The inevitable comparison of Walt Whitman and Isadora at once springs to the mind.

Like all great geniuses Isadora was practical. The things she visioned were true and right and therefore *possible*. But she had neither the patience nor the tact to cope with circumstances as they existed here. She was not a politician! Someone who understood fully her aims and ideas should have stood as interpreter between her and actual contact with worldly things; then perhaps America would have been able to profit by her vision.

Isadora's ideas about the Dance in relation to Drama were particularly interesting to me. She wanted to bring back the Dance to the Drama. She felt that one was incomplete without the other. One wonders what Wagner and Isadora together might not have accomplished. One of her dreams was to produce some of the Greek Dramas in conjunction with a great director in the Theatre. Most often she spoke of the *Bacchae* of Euripedes. She wanted to recreate the whole Bacchanale in the spirit of the Greek conception. What a marvellous thing it would have been; how terrible to think that life has been robbed of that, and so many other things equally beautiful that she visioned.

Why, instead of devoting millions to dead things had not someone the Faith to devote those millions to something ecstatically alive?

But that kind of life cannot die.

There is no death for Isadora Duncan.

The spirit and essence of her prophetic Vision will become a part of the Race itself. The world is different because she lived.

Those who saw her dance and had eyes to see, are different because she danced.

In the generations to come we will, in spite of ourselves, fulfill her prophecy.

"I see America dancing," she wrote, and by that she meant: "I see America free, generous, compassionate, tender, brave, with head up, looking toward the stars."

ISADORA DUNCAN

BY ROBERT EDMOND JONES

This great artist is no longer in our world. The sun has set: the cycle is finished.

In her art and in her life Isadora Duncan seemed to be an incarnation of all the energies of Nature. To see her dance was to realize the essence and soul of art. To know her was to see into a life that was varied and rich and vivid beyond all our imaginings of what life could be. Her spirit moved always in the center of a flame of creation, a flame that lifted up vast multitudes into its own radiance.

When Isadora Duncan appeared in Carnegie Hall for the last time she danced the Funeral March of Chopin, looking at us from beyond a great purple veil which she held in her outstretched arms. Now another veil, a veil of stillness and silence, has descended over this image of motion and music. We know that we shall never see her again. We are left with our memories.

We have put together between the covers of this book some of the words she set down from time to time about her work and her dreams. There are not many of these essays, but, like the flowers in the garland of Sappho, they are all roses.

THE ART OF THE DANCE

PHOTOGRAPH BY ARNOLD GENTHE

I SEE AMERICA DANCING

In one of his moments of prophetic love for America Walt Whitman said,
"I hear America singing," and I can imagine the mighty song that Walt heard, from the surge of the Pacific, over the plains, the Voices rising of the vast Choral of children, youths, men and women singing Democracy.

When I read this poem of Whitman's I, too, had a Vision: the Vision of America dancing a dance that would be the worthy expression of the song Walt heard when he heard America singing. This music would have a rhythm as great as the undulation, the swing or curves, of the Rocky Mountains. It would have nothing to do with the sensual tilting of the Jazz rhythm: it would be the vibration of the American soul striving upward through labour to Harmonious life. No more would this dance that I visioned have any vestige of the Fox Trot or the Charleston—rather would it be the living leap of the child springing toward the heights, toward its future accomplishment, toward a new great vision of life that would express America.

It has often caused me to smile, but somewhat bitterly, when people have called my dancing Greek. For I count its origin in the stories which my Irish Grandmother often told us of crossing the plains with Grandfather in '49 in a covered wagon—she eighteen, he twenty-one; and how her first child was born in such a wagon, during a famous battle with the Redskins. My grandfather, when the Indians were finally frightened away, put his head in at the door of the wagon, with smoking gun still in his hand, to greet his new-born child.

When they reached San Francisco, my grandfather built one of the first wooden houses; and I remember, when I was a little girl, visiting this same house, and my grandmother, remembering Ireland, used often to sing the Irish songs and dance the Irish jigs; only I fancy that into these Irish jigs had crept some of the heroic spirit of the Pioneer and the battles with the Redskins—probably some of the gestures of the Redskins themselves, and, again, a bit of Yankee Doodle when Grandfather Colonel Thomas Gray came marching home from the Civil War. All this Grandmother danced in the Irish Jig; and I learnt it from her, and put into it my own aspiration of Young America, and finally my great spiritual revelation of life from the lines of Walt Whitman. And that is the origin of the so-called Greek dance with which I have flooded the world.

That was the origin, the root. But afterwards, coming to Europe, I had three great Masters, the three great precursors of the Dance of our century—Beethoven, Nietzsche and Wagner. Beethoven created the Dance in mighty rhythm, Wagner in sculptural form, Nietzsche in Spirit. Nietzsche created the dancing philosopher.

I often wonder where is the American composer who will hear Walt's America singing, and who will compose the true music for the American Dance; which will contain no Jazz rhythm, no rhythm from the waist down; but from the solar plexus, the temporal home of the soul, upwards to the Star-Spangled Banner of the sky which arches over that great stretch of land from the Pacific, over the Plains, over the Sierra Nevadas, over the Rocky Mountains to the Atlantic.

I pray you, Young American Composer, create the music for the dance that shall express the America of Walt Whitman, the America of Abraham Lincoln.

It seems to me monstrous for anyone to believe that the Jazz rhythm expresses America. Jazz rhythm expresses the South African savage. America's music will be something different. It has yet to be written. No composer has yet caught the rhythm of America—it is too mighty for the ears of most. But some day it will gush forth from the great stretches of earth, rain down from the vast sky spaces of stars, and the American will be expressed in some mighty music that will shape its chaos to Harmony.

Long-legged strong boys and girls will dance to this music—not the tottering, ape-like convulsions of the Charleston, but a striking upward tremendous mounting, powerful mounting above the pyramids of Egypt, beyond the Parthenon of Greece, an expression of Beauty and Strength such as no civilization has ever known. That will be America dancing.

And this dance will have nothing in it either of the servile coquetry of the ballet or the sensual convulsion of the South African negro. It will be clean. I see America dancing, beautiful, strong, with one foot poised on the highest point of the Rockies, her two hands stretched out from the Atlantic to the Pacific, her fine head tossed to the sky, her forehead shining with a crown of a million stars.

How grotesque that they have encouraged in America schools of so-called bodily culture, of Swedish gymnastics, Dalcroze and the ballet. The real American type can never be a ballet dancer. The legs are too long, the body too supple and the spirit too free for this school of affected grace and toe-walking. It is noteworthy that all great ballet dancers have been very short women with small frames. A tall finely made woman could never dance the ballet. The type which expresses America at its finest could never dance the ballet. With the wildest turn of the imagination, you cannot picture the Goddess of Liberty dancing the ballet.

Then why accept this school in America?

Henry Ford has expressed the wish that all the children of Ford

City should dance. He also does not approve of the modern dances, but says let them dance the old-fashioned Waltz, Mazurka and Minuet. But the old-fashioned Waltz and Mazurka are an expression of sickly sentimentality and romance, which our youth has grown out of; and the Minuet is the expression of the unctuous servility of courtiers of the time of Louis XIV and of crinoline. What have these movements to do with the free youth of America? Doesn't Mr. Ford know that movements are as eloquent as words?

Why should our children bend the knee in that fastidious and servile dance, the Minuet, or twirl in the mazes of the false sentimentality of the Waltz? Rather let them come forth with great strides, leaps and bounds, with lifted forehead and far-spread arms, dancing the language of our pioneers, the fortitude of our heroes, the justice, kindness, purity of our women, and through it all the inspired love and tenderness of our mothers.

When the American children dance in this way, it will make of them Beautiful Beings worthy of the name of Democracy.

That will be America dancing.

© 1927.

THE PHILOSOPHER'S STONE OF DANCING

In music there are three sorts of composers: first, those who think out a scholarly music, who seek about and arrange, through their brains, a skillful and subtly effective score which appeals through the mind to the senses. Second, there are those who know how to translate their own emotions into the medium of sound, the joys and sorrows of their own hearts creating a music that appeals directly to the listener's heart, and brings tears by the memories it evokes of joys and sorrows, by the remembrance of happiness gone by. Third, there are those who, subconsciously, hear with their souls some melody of another world, and are able to express this in terms comprehensible and joyous to human ears.

There are likewise three kinds of dancers: first, those who consider dancing as a sort of gymnastic drill, made up of impersonal and graceful arabesques; second, those who, by concentrating their minds, lead the body into the rhythm of a desired emotion, expressing a remembered feeling or experience. And finally, there are those who convert the body into a luminous fluidity, surrendering it to the inspiration of the soul. This third sort of dancer understands that the body, by force of the soul, can in fact be converted to a luminous fluid. The flesh becomes light and transparent, as shown through the X-ray—but with the difference that the human soul is lighter than these rays. When, in its divine power, it completely possesses the body, it converts that into a luminous moving cloud and thus can manifest itself in the whole of its divinity. This is the explanation of the miracle of St. Francis walking on the sea. His body no longer weighed like ours, so light had it become through the soul.

Imagine then a dancer who, after long study, prayer and inspiration, has attained such a degree of understanding that his body is simply the luminous manifestation of his soul; whose body dances in accordance with a music heard inwardly, in an expression of something out of another, a profounder world. This is the truly creative dancer, natural but not imitative, speaking in movement out of himself and out of something greater than all selves.

So confident am I that the soul can be awakened, can completely possess the body, that when I have taken children into my schools I have aimed above all else to bring to them a consciousness of this power within themselves, of their relationship to the universal rhythm, to evoke from them the ecstasy, the beauty of this realization. The means to this awakening may be in part a revelation of the beauty of nature, and it may be in part that sort of music that the third group of composers gives us, that arises from and speaks to the soul.

There are perhaps grown people who have forgotten the language of the soul. But children understand. It is only necessary to say to them: "Listen to the music with *your soul*. Now, while you are listening, do you not feel an inner self awakening deep within you—that it is by its strength that your head is lifted, that your arms are raised, that you are walking slowly toward the light?"

This awakening is the first step in dancing, as I understand it.

When I began to dance with the movements and gestures my enraptured soul knew how to communicate to my body, others began to imitate me, not understanding that it was necessary to go back to a beginning, to find something in themselves first. In many theatres and schools I have seen these dancers, who comprehended only with the brain, who loaded down their dances with gestures; and their move-

PHOTOGRAPH BY ARNOLD GENTHE

PHOTOGRAPH BY ARNOLD GENTHE

ments seemed empty, dull and devoid of meaning. What they translated through the mind lacked all inspiration, all life. So, too, do those systems of dancing that are only arranged gymnastics, only too logically understood (Dalcroze, etc.). It seems to me criminal to entrust children, who cannot defend themselves, to this injurious training; for it is a crime to teach the child to guide his growing body by the stern power of the brain, while deadening impulse and inspiration.

The only power that can satisfactorily guide the child's body is the inspiration of the soul.

1920.

THE DANCE OF THE FUTURE

A WOMAN once asked me why I dance with bare feet and I replied, "Madam, I believe in the religion of the beauty of the human foot." The lady replied, "But I do not," and I said, "Yet you must, Madam, for the expression and intelligence of the human foot is one of the greatest triumphs of the evolution of man." "But," said the lady, "I do not believe in the evolution of man"; at this said I, "My task is at an end. I refer you to my most revered teachers, Mr. Charles Darwin and Mr. Ernst Haeckel." "But," said the lady, "I do not believe in Darwin and Haeckel." At this point I could think of nothing more to say. So you see that to convince people, I am of little value and ought not to speak. But I am brought from the seclusion of my study, trembling and stammering before a public and told to lecture on the dance of the future.

If we seek the real source of the dance, if we go to nature, we find that the dance of the future is the dance of the past, the dance of eternity, and has been and will always be the same.

The movement of waves, of winds, of the earth is ever in the same lasting harmony. We do not stand on the beach and inquire of the ocean what was its movement in the past and what will be its movement in the future. We realize that the movement peculiar to its nature is eternal to its nature. The movement of the free animals and birds remains always in correspondence to their nature, the necessities and wants of that nature, and its correspondence to the earth nature. It is only when you put free animals under false restrictions that they lose the power of moving in harmony with nature, and adopt a movement expressive of the restrictions placed about them.

So it has been with civilized man. The movements of the savage, who lived in freedom in constant touch with Nature, were unrestricted, natural and beautiful. Only the movements of the naked body can be perfectly natural. Man, arrived at the end of civilization, will have to return to nakedness, not to the unconscious nakedness of the savage, but to the conscious and acknowledged nakedness of the mature Man, whose body will be the harmonious expression of his spiritual being.

And the movements of this Man will be natural and beautiful like those of the free animals.

The movement of the universe concentrating in an individual becomes what is termed the will; for example, the movement of the earth, being the concentration of surrounding forces, gives to the earth its individuality, its will of movement. So creatures of the earth, receiving in turn these concentrating forces in their different relations, as transmitted to them through their ancestors and to those by the earth, in themselves evolve the movement of individuals which is termed the will.

The dance should simply be, then, the natural gravitation of this will of the individual, which in the end is no more nor less than a human translation of the gravitation of the universe.

The school of the ballet of today, vainly striving against the natural laws of gravitation or the natural will of the individual, and working in discord in its form and movement with the form and movement of nature, produces a sterile movement which gives no birth to future movements, but dies as it is made.

The expression of the modern school of ballet, wherein each action is an end, and no movement, pose or rhythm is successive or can be made to evolve succeeding action, is an expression of degeneration, of living death. All the movements of our modern ballet school are sterile movements because they are unnatural: their purpose is to create the delusion that the law of gravitation does not exist for them.

The primary or fundamental movements of the new school of the dance must have within them the seeds from which will evolve all other movements, each in turn to give birth to others in unending sequence of still higher and greater expression, thoughts and ideas.

To those who nevertheless still enjoy the movements, for historical or choreographic or whatever other reasons, to those I answer: They see no farther than the skirts and tricots. But look—under the skirts, under the tricots are dancing deformed muscles. Look still farther— underneath the muscles are deformed bones. A deformed skeleton is dancing before you. This deformation through incorrect dress and incorrect movement is the result of the training necessary to the ballet.

The ballet condemns itself by enforcing the deformation of the beautiful woman's body! No historical, no choreographic reasons can prevail against that!

It is the mission of all art to express the highest and most beautiful ideals of man. What ideal does the ballet express?

No, the dance was once the most noble of all arts; and it shall be again. From the great depth to which it has fallen, it shall be raised. The dancer of the future shall attain so great a height that all other arts shall be helped thereby.

To express what is the most moral, healthful and beautiful in art —this is the mission of the dancer, and to this I dedicate my life.

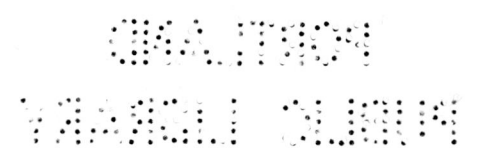

These flowers before me contain the dream of a dance; it could be named "The light falling on white flowers." A dance that would be a subtle translation of the light and the whiteness. So pure, so strong, that people would say: it is a soul we see moving, a soul that has reached the light and found the whiteness. We are glad it should move so. Through its human medium we have a satisfying sense of movement, of light and glad things. Through this human medium, the movement of all nature runs also through us, is transmitted to us from the dancer. We feel the movement of light intermingled with the thought of whiteness. It is a prayer, this dance; each movement reaches in long undulations to the heavens and becomes a part of the eternal rhythm of the spheres.

To find those primary movements for the human body from which shall evolve the movements of the future dance in ever-varying, natural, unending sequences, that is the duty of the new dancer of today.

As an example of this, we might take the pose of the Hermes of the Greeks. He is represented as flying on the wind. If the artist had pleased to pose his foot in a vertical position, he might have done so, as the God, flying on the wind, is not touching the earth; but realizing that no movement is true unless suggesting sequence of movements, the sculptor placed the Hermes with the ball of his foot resting on the wind, giving the movement an eternal quality.

In the same way I might make an example of each pose and gesture in the thousands of figures we have left to us on the Greek vases and bas-reliefs; there is not one which in its movement does not presuppose another movement.

This is because the Greeks were the greatest students of the laws of nature, wherein all is the expression of unending, ever-increasing evolution, wherein are no ends and no stops.

Such movements will always have to depend on and correspond to the form that is moving. The movements of a beetle correspond to its form. So do those of the horse. Even so the movements of the human body must correspond to its form. The dances of no two persons should be alike.

People have thought that so long as one danced in rhythm, the form and design did not matter; but no, one must perfectly correspond to the other. The Greeks understood this very well. There is a statuette that shows a dancing cupid. It is a child's dance. The movements of the plump little feet and arms are perfectly suited to its form. The sole of the foot rests flat on the ground, a position which might be ugly in a more developed person, but is natural in a child trying to keep its balance. One of the legs is half raised; if it were outstretched it would irritate us, because the movement would be unnatural. There is also a statue of a satyr in a dance that is quite different from that of the cupid. His movements are those of a ripe and muscular man. They are in perfect harmony with the structure of his body.

The Greeks in all their painting, sculpture, architecture, literature, dance and tragedy evolved their movements from the movement of nature, as we plainly see expressed in all representations of the Greek gods, who, being no other than the representatives of natural forces, are always designed in a pose expressing the concentration and evolution of these forces. This is why the art of the Greeks is not a national or characteristic art but has been and will be the art of all humanity for all time.

Therefore dancing naked upon the earth I naturally fall into Greek positions, for Greek positions are only earth positions.

The noblest in art is the nude. This truth is recognized by all, and followed by painters, sculptors and poets; only the dancer has forgotten it, who should most remember it, as the instrument of her art is the human body itself.

Man's first conception of beauty is gained from the form and symmetry of the human body. The new school of the dance should begin with that movement which is in harmony with and will develop the highest form of the human body.

I intend to work for this dance of the future. I do not know whether I have the necessary qualities: I may have neither genius nor talent nor temperament. But I know that I have a Will; and will and energy sometimes prove greater than either genius or talent or temperament.

Let me anticipate all that can be said against my qualification for my work, in the following little fable:

The Gods looked down through the glass roof of my studio and Athene said, "She is not wise, she is not wise, in fact, she is remarkably stupid."

And Demeter looked and said, "She is a weakling; a little thing —not like my deep-breasted daughters who play in the fields of Eleusis; one can see each rib; she is not worthy to dance on my broad-wayed Earth." And Iris looked down and said, "See how heavily she moves—does she guess nothing of the swift and gracious movement of a winged being?" And Pan looked and said, "What? Does she think she knows aught of the movements of my satyrs, splendid ivy-horned fellows who have within them all the fragrant life of the woods and waters?" And then Terpsichore gave one scornful glance; "And she calls that dancing! Why, her feet move more like the lazy steps of a deranged turtle."

And all the Gods laughed; but I looked bravely up through the glass roof and said: "O ye immortal Gods, who dwell in high Olympus and live on Ambrosia and Honey-cakes, and pay no studio rent nor bakers' bills thereof, do not judge me so scornfully. It is true, O Athene, that I am not wise, and my head is a rattled institution; but I do occasionally read the word of those who have gazed into the infinite blue of thine eyes, and I bow my empty gourd head very humbly before thine altars. And, O Demeter of the Holy Garland," I continued, "it is true that the beautiful maidens of your broad-wayed earth would not admit me of their company; still I have thrown aside my sandals that my feet may touch your life-giving earth more reverently, and I have had your sacred Hymn sung before the present day Barbarians, and I have made them to listen and to find it good.

"And, O Iris of the golden wings, it is true that mine is but a sluggish movement; others of my profession have luted more violently against the laws of gravitation, from which laws, O glorious one, you are alone exempt. Yet the wind from your wings has swept through my poor earthy spirit, and I have often brought prayers to your courage-inspiring image.

"And, O Pan, you who were pitiful and gentle to simple Psyche in her wanderings, think more kindly of my little attempts to dance in your woody places.

"And you most exquisite one, Terpsichore, send to me a little comfort and strength that I may proclaim your power on Earth during my life; and afterwards, in the shadowy Hades, my wistful spirit shall dance dances better yet in thine honour."

Then came the voice of Zeus, the Thunderer:

"Continue your way and rely upon the eternal justice of the immortal Gods; if you work well they shall know of it and be pleased thereof."

In this sense, then, I intend to work, and if I could find in my dance a few or even one single position that the sculptor could transfer into marble so that it might be preserved, my work would not have been in vain; this one form would be a gain; it would be a first step for the future. My intention is, in due time, to found a school, to build a theatre where a hundred little girls shall be trained in my art, which they, in their turn, will better. In this school I shall not teach the children to imitate my movements, but to make their own. I shall not force them to study certain definite movements; I shall help them to develop those movements which are natural to them. Whosoever sees the movements of an untaught little child cannot deny that its movements are beautiful. They are beautiful because they are natural to the child. Even so the movements of the human body may be beautiful in every stage of development so long as they are in harmony with that stage and degree of maturity which the body has attained. There will always be movements which are the perfect expression of that individual body and that individual soul; so we must not force it to make movements which are not natural to it but which belong to a school. An intelligent child must be astonished to find that in the ballet school it is taught movements contrary to all those movements which it would make of its own accord.

This may seem a question of little importance, a question of differing opinions on the ballet and the new dance. But it is a great question. It is not only a question of true art, it is a question of race, of the development of the female sex to beauty and health, of the return to the original strength and to natural movements of woman's body. It is a question of the development of perfect mothers and the birth of healthy and beautiful children. The dancing school of the future is to develop and to show the ideal form of woman. It will be, as it were, a museum of the living beauty of the period.

Travellers coming into a country and seeing the dancers should find in them that country's ideal of the beauty of form and movement. But strangers who today come to any country, and there see the dancers of the ballet school, would get a strange notion indeed of the ideal of beauty in that country. More than this, dancing like any art of any time should reflect the highest point the spirit of mankind has reached in that special period. Does anybody think that the present day ballet school expresses this?

Why are its positions in such contrast to the beautiful positions of the antique sculptures which we preserve in our museums and which are constantly presented to us as perfect models of ideal beauty? Or have our museums been founded only out of historical and archaeological interest, and not for the sake of the beauty of the objects which they contain?

The ideal of beauty of the human body cannot change with fashion but only with evolution. Remember the story of the beautiful sculpture of a Roman girl which was discovered under the reign of Pope Innocent VIII, and which by its beauty created such a sensation that the men thronged to see it and made pilgrimages to it as to a holy shrine, so that the Pope, troubled by the movement which it originated, finally had it buried again.

And here I want to avoid a misunderstanding that might easily arise. From what I have said you might conclude that my intention is to return to the dances of the old Greeks, or that I think that the dance of the future will be a revival of the antique dances or even of those of the primitive tribes. No, the dance of the future will be a new movement, a consequence of the entire evolution which mankind has passed through. To return to the dances of the Greeks would be as impossible as it is unnecessary. We are not Greeks and therefore cannot dance Greek dances.

But the dance of the future will have to become again a high religious art as it was with the Greeks. For art which is not religious is not art, is mere merchandise.

The dancer of the future will be one whose body and soul have grown so harmoniously together that the natural language of that soul will have become the movement of the body. The dancer will not belong to a nation but to all humanity. She will dance not in the form

PHOTOGRAPH BY ARNOLD GENTHE

PHOTOGRAPH BY ARNOLD GENTHE

of nymph, nor fairy, nor coquette, but in the form of woman in her greatest and purest expression. She will realize the mission of woman's body and the holiness of all its parts. She will dance the changing life of nature, showing how each part is transformed into the other. From all parts of her body shall shine radiant intelligence, bringing to the world the message of the thoughts and aspirations of thousands of women. She shall dance the freedom of woman.

Oh, what a field is here awaiting her! Do you not feel that she is near, that she is coming, this dancer of the future! She will help womankind to a new knowledge of the possible strength and beauty of their bodies, and the relation of their bodies to the earth nature and to the children of the future. She will dance the body emerging again from centuries of civilized forgetfulness, emerging not in the nudity of primitive man, but in a new nakedness, no longer at war with spirituality and intelligence, but joining with them in a glorious harmony.

This is the mission of the dancer of the future. Oh, do you not feel that she is near, do you not long for her coming as I do? Let us prepare the place for her. I would build for her a temple to await her. Perhaps she is yet unborn, perhaps she is now a little child. Perhaps, oh blissful! it may be my holy mission to guide her first steps, to watch the progress of her movements day by day until, far outgrowing my poor teaching, her movements will become godlike, mirroring in themselves the waves, the winds, the movements of growing things, the flight of birds, the passing of clouds, and finally the thought of man in his relation to the universe.

Oh, she is coming, the dancer of the future: the free spirit, who will inhabit the body of new woman; more glorious than any woman that has yet been; more beautiful than the Egyptian, than the Greek, the early Italian, than all women of past centuries—the highest intelligence in the freest body!

1902 *or* 1903. © 1909.

THE PARTHENON

Anyone who, arriving at the foot of the Acropolis, has mounted with prayerful feet toward the Parthenon, and at length standing before this monument of the one immortal Beauty, feeling his soul lifting towards this glorious form, realizing that he has gained that secret middle place from which radiate in vast circles all knowledge and all Beauty—and that he has arrived at the core and root of this beauty—who, lifting his eyes to the rhythmical succession of Doric columns, has felt "form" in its finest and noblest sense fulfill the spirit's highest want of form, that one will understand for what I am striving in my first dance tonight. It is my effort to express the feeling of the human body in relation to the Doric column.

For the last four months, each day I have stood before this miracle of perfection wrought of human hands. I have seen around it sloping the Hills, in many forms, but in direct contrast to them the Parthenon, expressing their fundamental idea. Not in imitation of the outside forms of nature, but in understanding of nature's great secret rules, rise the Doric columns.

The first days as I stood there my body was as nothing and my soul was scattered; but gradually called by the great inner voice of the Temple, came back the parts of my self to worship it: first came my soul and looked upon the Doric columns, and then came my body and looked—but in both were silence and stillness, and I did not dare to move, for I realized that of all the movements my body had made none was worthy to be made before a Doric Temple. And as I stood thus I realized that I must find a dance whose effort was to be worthy of this Temple—or never dance again.

Neither Satyr nor Nymph had entered here, neither Shadows nor Bacchantes. All that I had danced was forbidden this Temple—neither love nor hate nor fear, nor joy nor sorrow—only a rhythmic cadence, those Doric columns—only in perfect harmony this glorious Temple, calm through all the ages.

For many days no movement came to me. And then one day came the thought: These columns which seem so straight and still are not really straight, each one is curving gently from the base to the height, each one is in flowing movement, never resting, and the movement of each is in harmony with the others. And as I thought this my arms rose slowly toward the Temple and I leaned forward—and then I knew I had found my dance, and it was a Prayer.

1903 *or* 1904.

THE DANCER AND NATURE

IN NO country is the soul made so sensible of Beauty and of Wisdom as in Greece. Gazing at the sky one knows why Athene, the Goddess of Wisdom, was called "the Blue-Eyed One," and why learning and beauty are always joined in her service. And one feels also why Greece has been the land of great philosophers, lovers of wisdom, and why the greatest of these has called the highest beauty the highest wisdom. . . .

Does the recognition of Beauty as the highest Idea belong wholly to the province of Man's Intellect? . . . Or do you think that a woman might also attain to a knowledge of the highest beauty? Considering women in our country as they are today, does it not seem that very few among them have a true feeling and love for beauty as an Idea? Does it not seem they have recognition of that which is trifling and pretty only, but are blind to true beauty?

At the words "true beauty" there comes before my eyes a procession of figures, women's figures, draped lightly in noble draperies. They go two and two, and the harmony of their bodies swaying to their steps is like music. . . .

One might well be led to believe that women are incapable of knowing beauty as an Idea, but I think this only seems so, not because they are incapable of perceiving but only because they are at present blind to the chief means in their power of understanding True Beauty. Through the eyes beauty most readily finds a way to the soul, but there is another way for women—perhaps an easier way—and that is through the knowledge of their own bodies.

The human body has through all ages itself been the symbol of highest beauty. I see a young goatherd sitting surrounded by his flock, and before him, rose-tipped of the sun, stands the Goddess of Cyprus, and she smiles as she reaches her hand for the prize which she knows to be hers. That exquisitely poised head, those shoulders gently sloping, those breasts firm and round, the ample waist with its free lines, curving to the hips, down to the knees and feet—all one perfect whole.

The artist without this first consciousness of proportion and line of the human form could have had no consciousness of the beauty surrounding him. When his ideal of the human form is a noble one, then his conception of all line and form in Nature is noblest: the knowledge of sky and earth forms—and from this the conception of line and form of architecture, painting and sculpture. All art—does it not come originally from the first human consciousness of the nobility of the lines of the human body?

How shall woman attain a knowledge of this beauty? Shall she find this knowledge in the gymnasium examining her muscles, in the museum regarding the sculptured forms, or by the continual contemplation of beautiful objects, and the reflection of them in the mind? These are all ways, but the chief thing is, she must *live* this beauty, and her body must be the living exponent of it.

Not by the thought or contemplation of beauty only, but by the living of it, will woman learn. And as form and movement are inseparable, I might say that she will learn by that movement which is in accordance with the beautiful form.

And how shall one name that movement which is in accord with the most beautiful human form? There is a name, the name of one of the oldest of the arts—time-honored as one of the nine Muses—but it is a name that has fallen into such disrepute in our day that it has come to mean just the opposite of this definition. I would name it the Dance. Woman is to learn beauty of form and movement through the dance.

I believe here is a wonderful undiscovered inheritance for coming womanhood, the old dance which is to become the new. She shall be sculpture not in clay or marble but in her own body which she shall endeavor to bring to the highest state of plastic beauty; she shall be painter, but, as part of a great picture, she shall mingle in many groups of new changing light and color. With the movement of her body she shall find the secret of perfect proportion of line and curve. The art of the dance she will hold as a great well-spring of new life for sculpture, painting and architecture.

Before woman can reach high things in the art of the dance, dancing must exist as an art for her to practice, which at the present day in our country it certainly does not.

Where are we to look for the great fountain-head of movement? Woman is not a thing apart and separate from all other life organic and inorganic. She is but a link in the chain, and her movement must be one with the great movement which runs through the universe; and therefore the fountain-head for the art of the dance will be the study of the movements of Nature.

With the strengthening of the breeze over the seas, the waters form in long undulations. Of all movement which gives us delight and satisfies the soul's sense of movement, that of the waves of the sea seems to me the finest. This great wave movement runs through all Nature, for when we look over the waters to the long line of hills on the shore, they seem also to have the great undulating movement of the sea; and all movements in Nature seem to me to have as their ground-plan the law of wave movement.

Yesterday we were speaking of the movement in Nature, saying that the wave movement was the great foundation. The idea continually presents itself to me, and I see waves rising through all things. Looking through the trees they seem also to be a pattern conforming to lines of waves. We might think of them from another standpoint: that all energy expresses itself through this wave movement. For does not sound travel in waves, and light also? And when we come to the movements of organic nature, it would seem that all free natural movements conform to the law of wave movement: the flight of birds, for instance, or the bounding of animals. It is the alternate attraction and resistance of the law of gravity that causes this wave movement.

I see dance motifs in all things about me. All true dance movements possible to the human body exist primarily in Nature. What is "true dance" in opposition to what might be named the false dance? The true dance is appropriate to the most beautiful human form; the false dance is the opposite of this definition—that is, that movement which conforms to a deformed human body. First draw me the form of a woman as it is in Nature. And now draw me the form of a woman in a modern corset and the satin slippers used by our modern dancers. Now do you not see that the movement that would conform to one figure would be perfectly impossible for the other? To the first all the rhythmic movements that run through Nature would be possible. They would find this form their natural medium for movement. To the second figure these movements would be impossible on account of the rhythm being broken, and stopped at the extremities.

We cannot take movements for the second figure from Nature, but must on the contrary go according to set geometrical figures based on straight lines; and that is exactly what the school of dance of our day has done. They have invented a movement which conforms admirably to the human figure of the second illustration, but which would be impossible to the figure as drawn in our first sketch. Therefore it is only those movements which would be natural to the first figure that I call the true dance.

What I name as "deformed" is by many people held to be an evolution in form to something higher, and the dance which would be appropriate to woman's natural form would be held by them as primitive and uncultivated. Whereas they would name the dance which is appropriate to the form much improved, compressed in corsets and shoes, as the dance appropriate to the culture of the present day. How would one answer these people?

That man's culture is the making use of Nature's forces in channels harmonious to those forces, and never the going directly against Nature and all art intimately connected with Nature at its roots; that the painter, the poet, the sculptor and the dramatist do but fix for us through their work according to their ability to observe in Nature; that Nature always has been and must be the great source of all art; and that there is a complete separation of the dancer's movement from the movement of Nature. . . .

Probably 1905.

WHAT DANCING SHOULD BE

I was sitting in my study this afternoon, regarding by the light of the dying day some little figures on my book-shelf, a Satyr, a Nymph, an Amazon, an Eros; and the movement of each was different, and the movement of each was beautiful. Why beautiful? Because the movement of each was in direct correspondence with the form and symmetry of each; therefore the form and the movement were one. I was regarding these figures in turn, and my enjoyment of the harmonies in their lines was like that of listening to music, when the door opened, and quite unannounced a little girl came in. She ran to me, and throwing her arms about me, cried, "Dear sweet Miss Duncan, I liked your dance so much, I must come and see you."

I regarded the glowing life in the face of the child. Something there seemed familiar to me. What was it? Unconsciously I raised my eyes to the shelf where danced my fauns and nymphs. Was it not there, the resemblance? The eternal childhood of the world? The Golden Age, does it not live again, in all ages in all children?

"And why do you find my dance beautiful, little one?" I asked.

"Because it is so natural," answered the child.

"And," I said, "are all natural things beautiful?" for I would learn from the child a definition of beauty; and the child answered gladly, "Yes!"

O wise little philosopher, who answers from the sureness of instinct, without need of consideration! Yes, for Beauty is the soul and the laws of the Universe, and all that is in accordance with this soul and these laws is Beauty. And ugliness is only that which is against the harmony of these laws. . . .

The dance and sculpture are the two arts most closely united, and the foundation of both is Nature. The sculptor and the dancer both have to seek in Nature the most beautiful forms, and the movements which inevitably express the spirit of those forms. So the teaching of sculpture and of the dance ought to go hand in hand. The sculptor may interpret the movements and the forms imaginatively, but only the study of Nature can serve as a foundation. The study of living figures that dance spontaneously, each an expression of an individual soul, of its deepest understanding and personal power, is what the school should offer the sculptor, and what I wish to bring about. . . .

Must the sculptor draw all from his imagination, or from the memory of what is left to us from Greek art? I say that is not sufficient for inspiration—for a great living work. Now where shall the sculptor of today find beautiful living forms in rhythmic movement? Let him leave his studio and his model and go to the opera, to see the school of the dance as represented by the national ballet: let him go pencil and paper in hand, and then let him tell us whether he has found one pose, one movement, one suggestion for the beauty of free woman's body in the expression of the highest beauty, one feeling which would inspire an art work of purity and holiness.

So I say that the relation of the new school of the dance to sculpture is to be a very close one. From its earliest stages, when the little ones begin their first childish movements, we will have days when every sculptor who asks shall be admitted to study the free unconscious movements of the children without clothes. And as gradually the movements of the little girls develop and become full, rhythmical and beautiful, they will be more and more a source of light for sculptors.

CRAYON DRAWING BY VAN DEERING PERRINE

Courtesy Mr. A. C. Goodyear

DRAWING BY ANDRÉ DUNOYER DE SEGONZAC

Have you ever seen the little girls who are studying in the ballet of today? The little girls sweet, bright and graceful—but their feet are being tortured into deformed shapes. Their tender little bodies already are being forced into tight bodices and baby corsets, while their natural graceful movements are being tormented into unnatural straight kickings of the legs, toe walking, and all sorts of awkward contortions which are directly contrary to what a child's natural movement would be if developed in the line of reason and beauty.

I witnessed such a children's ballet once at the Berlin Opera House, and I say it is a shame and a disgrace to the intelligence of the German nation. Now whence does this style of dancing come? It comes from France, from the time of the most polluted of courts, and I say it suited the falseness and shallowness of those courts perfectly, but it does not suit our time, and it does not find itself at home in a nation in which Schiller and Goethe and Richard Wagner and many other great and beautiful souls have written what real dancing should be.

What dancing should be—how many poets, how many philosophers, how many scientists of Germany have written beautiful lines on this subject! And they have mostly written of little children dancing, or of maidens dancing, or of one woman dancing. And when one reads such lines, it is like a call from the depths of their poet-souls: "O Woman, come before us, before our eyes longing for beauty, and tired of the ugliness of this civilization, come in simple tunics, letting us see the line and harmony of the body beneath, and dance for us. Dance us the sweetness of life and its meanings, dance for us the movements of birds, the waters, waving trees, floating clouds, dance for us the holiness and beauty of woman's body."

Like a call it has come from the souls of these great ones to women: "Give us again the sweetness and beauty of the true dance, give us again the joy of seeing the simple unconscious pure body of woman." Like a great call it has come, and women must hear and answer it.

A CHILD DANCING

Seated on the beach at Noordwijk, I look on while my little niece, who has come to visit me, from the Grünewald School, dances here before the waves. I gaze across the vast expanse of surging water—wave after wave streaming endlessly past, throwing up the white foam. And in front of it all the dainty little figure in her white fluttering dress, dancing before the monstrous sea! And I feel as though the heart-beat of her little life were sounding in unison with the mighty life of the water, as though it possessed something of the same rhythm, something of the same life, and my heart rejoices at her dancing.

For a long time I am lost in contemplation, and her dance by the sea seems to me to contain in little the whole problem on which I am working. It seems to reflect the naturally beautiful motions of the human body, in the dance. She dances because she is full of the joy of life. She dances because the waves are dancing before her eyes, because the winds are dancing, because she can feel the rhythm of the dance throughout the whole of nature. To her it is a joy to dance; to me it is a joy to watch her. It is summer now, here by the sea, and life is filled with joy; but I think of winter, in the towns, in the streets, in the houses, of life in the towns in the gloomy winter. How can the life of nature, the joy of summer, of sunshine, the joy of a child dancing by the sea, how can all this beauty be drawn into life, into the towns? Can the dancer suggest all this and remind men of it in the winter time, in the cities? Can she call up within me the same delight which she is giving me now as I sit here on the beach and watch her dancing?

I look more closely and study her movements. What is this dance she is dancing? I see that the simple movements and steps are those she has learnt in our school during the past two years. But she invests them with her own spontaneous child-like feelings, her own child-like happiness. She is only dancing what she has been taught, but the movements taught her are so completely in harmony with her child-like nature that they seem to spring direct from her inmost being.

In the memoranda for my method of instruction I have laid it down that:—

"The child must not be taught to make movements, but her soul, as it grows to maturity must be guided and instructed; in other words, the body must be taught to express itself by means of the motions which are natural to it. We do not allow the child to make a single movement unless it knows why it makes it. I do not mean to say that the meaning of every motion must be explained to the child in words, but that the motion must be of such a nature that the child feels the reason for it in every fibre. In this way the child will become versed in the simple language of gestures."

These first memoranda in my notebook come back to my memory as I sit here watching Temple dancing on the beach. Her dancing is, in a sense, an epitome of all the hopes and all the efforts I have expended on my school since its foundation.

I can picture to myself the smile of amusement with which some learned professor of the history of dancing will read these simple lines. He will doubtless begin with a long dissertation on the history of dancing in every country and age. He will prove conclusively that the art of dancing cannot be acquired either in the woods, or by the seashore, and that it would be madness to found a school in the belief that it was possible. But if we are to bring about a renaissance of the art of dancing, it will not spring from the head of any learned professor, but will rather bud forth from the joyous movements of children's bodies, guided by the flute of the great god Pan himself.

1906.

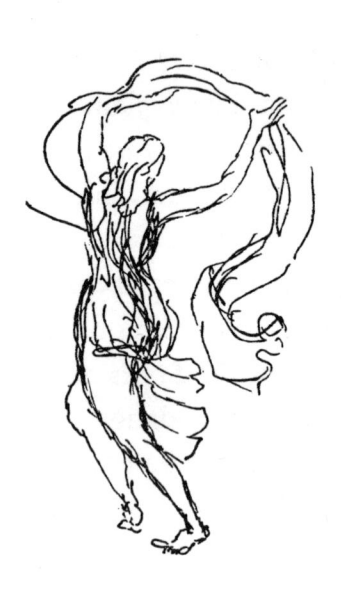

MOVEMENT IS LIFE

STUDY the movement of the earth, the movement of plants and trees, of animals, the movement of winds and waves—and then study the movements of a child. You will find that the movement of all natural things works within harmonious expression. And this is true in the first years of a child's life; but very soon the movement is imposed from without by wrong theories of education, and the child soon loses its natural spontaneous life, and its power of expressing that in movement.

I notice that a baby of three or four coming to my school is responsive to the exaltation of beautiful music, whereas a child of eight or nine is already under the influence of a conventional and mechanical conception of life imposed upon it by the pedagogues. The child of nine has already entered into the prison of conventional and mechanical movement, in which it will remain and suffer its entire life, until advancing age brings on paralysis of bodily expression.

When asked for the pedagogic program of my school, I reply: "Let us first teach little children to breathe, to vibrate, to feel, and to become one with the general harmony and movement of nature. Let us first produce a beautiful human being, a dancing child." Nietzsche has said that he cannot believe in a god that cannot dance. He has also said, "Let that day be considered lost on which we have not danced."

But he did not mean the execution of pirouettes. He meant the exaltation of life in movement.

The harmony of music exists equally with the harmony of movement in nature.

Man has not invented the harmony of music. It is one of the underlying principles of life. Neither could the harmony of movement be invented: it is essential to draw one's conception of it from Nature herself, and to seek the rhythm of human movement from the rhythm of water in motion, from the blowing of the winds on the world, in all the earth's movements, in the motions of animals, fish, birds, reptiles, and even in primitive man, whose body still moved in harmony with nature.

With the first conception of a conscience, man became self-conscious, lost the natural movements of the body; today in the light of intelligence gained through years of civilization, it is essential that he consciously seek what he has unconsciously lost.

All the movements of the earth follow the lines of wave motion. Both sound and light travel in waves. The motion of water, winds, trees and plants progresses in waves. The flight of a bird and the movements of all animals follow lines like undulating waves. If then one seeks a point of physical beginning for the movement of the human body, there is a clue in the undulating motion of the wave. It is one of the elemental facts of nature, and out of such elementals the child, the dancer, absorbs something basic to dancing.

The human being too is a source. Dancing expresses in a different language, different from nature, the beauty of the body; and the body grows more beautiful with dancing. All the conscious art of mankind has grown out of the discovery of the natural beauty of the human body. Men tried to reproduce it in sand or on a wall, and painting thus was born. From our understanding of the harmonies and proportions of the members of the body sprang architecture. From the wish to glorify the body sculpture was created.

The beauty of the human form is not chance. One cannot change it by dress. The Chinese women deformed their feet with tiny shoes; women of the time of Louis XIV deformed their bodies with corsets; but the ideal of the human body must forever remain the same. The Venus of Milo stands on her pedestal in the Louvre for an ideal; women pass before her, hurt and deformed by the dress of ridiculous fashions; she remains forever the same, for she is beauty, life, truth.

It is because the human form is not and cannot be at the mercy of fashion or the taste of an epoch that the beauty of woman is eternal. It is the guide of human evolution toward the goal of the human race, toward the ideal of the future which dreams of becoming God.

The architect, the sculptor, the painter, the musician, the poet, all understand how the idealization of the human form and the consciousness of its divinity are at the root of all art created by man. A single artist has lost this divinity, an artist who above all should be the first to desire it—the dancer.

Dancing, indeed, through a long era lacked all sense of elemental natural movement. It tried to afford the sense of gravity overcome—a denial of nature. Its movements were not living, flowing, undulating, giving rise inevitably to other movements. All freedom and spontaneity were lost in a maze of intricate artifice. The dancer had to be dressed up artificially to be in keeping with its unnatural character.

Then when I opened the door to nature again, revealing a different kind of dance, some people explained it all by saying, "See, it is *natural* dancing." But with its freedom, its accordance with natural movement, there was always design too—even in nature you find sure, even rigid design. "Natural" dancing should mean only that the dance never goes against nature, not that anything is left to chance.

Nature must be the source of all art, and dance must make use of nature's forces in harmony and rhythm, but the dancer's movement will always be separate from any movement in nature.

Probably 1909.

BEAUTY AND EXERCISE

Many years ago the idea came to me that it might be possible to bring up young girls in such an atmosphere of beauty that, in setting continually before their eyes an ideal figure, their own bodies would grow to be the personification of this figure; and that through continual emulation of it and by the perpetual practice of beautiful movements, they would become perfect in form and gesture. This has long appeared to me to be the type of the ideal school of dancing.

Having in mind, as I have said before, that form and movement are one, I thought it necessary for the culture of beautiful movement to tend as carefully the growing figures of my pupils as a gardener tends the shapes of his fruit and flowers.

With this aim I placed in my schools different ideal representations of the female form, taking even those of the very first years—bas-reliefs and sculptures of dancing children, books and paintings showing the child form as it was dreamed of by the painters and sculptors of every age; paintings of dancing children on Greek vases; little Tanagra and Bœotian figures; Donatello's group of dancing children, which is a radiant childish melody; Gainsborough's Dancing Children.

All these figures have a certain fraternity in the naive grace of their form and movement, as if the children of every age met and joined hands through the centuries. The real children of the schools, moving and dancing amidst them, must resemble them, must reflect unconsciously, in their forms and movements, a little of this infantile joy and grace. And that is a first step towards growth in beauty, the first step of the new dance.

I also place in my schools figures of young girls dancing, running, jumping, those young Spartan girls who, in the gymnasiums, were trained to hard exercises, so that they might become the mothers of heroic warriors, those light runners who took part in the annual games, exquisite terra-cotta figures with flying veils and floating garments; young girls dancing hand-in-hand at the Panatheneas. They represent the aim to be attained by the pupils of my schools, who soon learn to feel an intimate love for these figures, and in trying each day to resemble them are permeated with the secret of their harmony. For I believe that it is only by awakening a strong wish for beauty that beauty can be obtained.

To attain this harmony they must every day do special exercises chosen for the purpose. But these exercises are chosen so as to coincide with their own will, so that they are accomplished with good humor and eagerness. Each one of them is not only a means to an end, but an end in itself, and this end is to make perfect and happy each day of life.

The purpose of these daily exercises is to make of the body at each period of its development an instrument as perfect as possible, an instrument for the expression of that harmony which, permeating everything, is ready to flow into bodies which have been prepared for it. The exercises begin by a simple gymnastic preparation of the muscles to make them strong and flexible; the first dancing steps only begin after these gymnastic exercises are completed. They consist at first of a simple rhythmic walk, learning to walk slowly to the sounds of a simple rhythm, then to walk quicker to the sound of more complicated rhythms, then to run, at first slowly, then to jump lightly at a certain moment of the rhythm.

By means of these exercises the pupils learn to read the notes on the scale of movement as the notes of music are learnt on the scale of sound. Later, these notes can be made to harmonize with the most various and subtle compositions. But these daily exercises are only one part of the studies. The pupils, always dressed in free and graceful draperies during their sports, in the playing fields, during their walks or in the woods, run and jump naturally until they have learned to express themselves by movement as easily as others can express themselves by word or song.

Their studies and observations are not limited to the forms of art, but are specially directed towards the movements of nature. The movements of the clouds in the wind, the waving of trees, the flight of birds, the whirling of leaves, all have a special signification for them. They learn to observe the special quality of each movement. They develop a secret sympathy in their souls, unknown to others, which makes them comprehend these movements as most people cannot. For every fiber of their bodies, sensitive and alert, responds to the melody of Nature and sings with her.

How often, returning from these studies, coming to the dance room, have these pupils felt in their bodies an irresistible impulse to dance out one or another movement which they had just observed! A Dionysian emotion possesses them.

And thus in time, I think, some of them will come to the composition of their own dances. But even when they are dancing together, each one, while forming part of a whole, under group inspiration, will preserve a creative individuality. And all the parts together will compose a unified harmony that will bring a new birth to the world: will make live again the flaming beauty of the dramatic Chorus, the Chorus of tragedy, the eternal hymn of the struggle between man and Destiny.

The culture of the form and movement of the body is practised today in two ways: by gymnastics and by dancing. Both should go together, for without gymnastics, without the healthy and methodical development of the body, the real dance is unattainable. Gymnastics should form the basis of all physical education; the body must be given plenty of light and air; its development must be carried out methodically; the whole vital strength of the body must be brought to its full expansion. This is the business of the professor of gymnastics. Then comes dancing. Into a body that has been harmoniously developed and brought to its highest degree of energy, the spirit of dancing enters. Movement and culture of his body form the aim of the gymnast; for the dancer they are only the means. Thus, the body itself must be forgotten, for it is only a harmonious and well adapted instrument whose movements express not only the movements of the body, as in gymnastics, but also the thoughts and feelings of a soul.

THE DANCE IN RELATION TO TRAGEDY

THE DANCE of the past reached its highest point when it formed the Chorus of Greek tragedy. At the sublime moment of the tragedy, when sorrow and suffering were most acute, the Chorus would appear. Then the soul of the audience, harrowed to the point of agony, was restored to harmony by the elemental rhythms of song and movement. The Chorus gave to the audience the fortitude to support those moments that otherwise would have been too terrible for human endurance.

This is the highest aim and object of dancing. To take its legitimate place in tragedy with music and poetry, to be the intermediary between the tragedy and the audience, creating complete harmony between them.

My work for the dance has always had this end in view, this light has always been before me: to restore the dance to its true place as Chorus, the very soul of tragedy. Up to a very short time ago dancing in the modern theatre was conceived as a sort of interlude, a pleasant filler, far removed from a living *rapprochement* with drama. It was in 1898, while studying Glück's music, that I seemed to have discovered the bridge that would restore the dance to its true sphere. Glück better than anyone else understood the Greek Chorus, its rhythm, the grave beauty of its movements, the great impersonality of its soul, stirred, but never despairing.

I studied the movements for choruses and dances in the works of

ISADORA DUNCAN DANCING GLÜCK'S ORPHÉE

CHALK DRAWING BY GRANDJOUAN

ISADORA DUNCAN DANCING A SCHUBERT MOMENT MUSICALE

CHALK DRAWING BY GRANDJOUAN

Glück with the desire to draw the movements of dancing nearer to the intent of the Chorus in a tragedy. It has been objected that this was never Glück's intention. I differ from that opinion. Glück often spoke in passionate terms of sincere movements, of true gesture. He pleaded for nature, and though he wrote for the ballets of his day, I am sure it was the gracious image of bodies moving freely, of garments blown about by the wind, that inspired him. He knew the Greek vases: he must have been influenced by their running, leaping figures. And so, in dancing the choruses and dances of *Orpheus,* I do not try to represent Orpheus or Eurydice, but the plastic movements of the Chorus, the tragic Chorus.

THE GREEK THEATRE

THE GREEK theatre was built not for the audience, but for the artist, with whom the audience was only too pleased to collaborate. The Greek theatre, moreover, represented a collaboration between the architect, the dramatist and the theatre artists.

The architect said to the dramatist, "What form of theatre do you wish for your work?" and the dramatist replied, "That form in which the greatest number of people can see, hear and feel at the same moment with the same intensity and equal proportions."

The architect said to the dancer, "What form?" and the dancer, spreading his arms in a great circle, replied "That form which enables me to take a vast audience into my arms—the form of theatre in which all the people sitting there will feel the significance of a simple gesture in equal vision of form and proportion—a form of theatre in which my magnetic force can go forth from me covering the people in uninterrupted rays as the sun's light covers the earth."

And to the actor: "What form of theatre?" The actor replied: "That form in which a simple tone of my voice, going on the natural currents of its sound waves, will stir the hearts of a vast multitude sitting before me in places one not more fortunate than the others; in which the emotion I give will flow from one to another—infectious, all-compelling waves of emotion going from me to them and returning to me."

And so was the Greek theatre built. There were no "boxes," no gallery, no balconies, no parquette. The Greek was essentially a democratic theatre. As artists are the priests of a religion, so all people before a great art manifestation should be equal.

Greek tragedy sprang from the dancing and singing of the first Greek Chorus. Dancing has gone a long way astray. She must return to her original place—hand in hand with the Muses encircling Apollo. She must become again the primitive Chorus, and the drama will be reborn from her inspiration. Then she will again take her place as the sister art of tragedy, she will spring from music—the great, impersonal, eternal and divine wellspring of art.

1915.

EDUCATION AND THE DANCE

THE SCHOOL of the dance should have two aims or visions. One of these is of the earth and the other is of production. In forming my school I had primarily in mind the aim to contribute this most important discovery to the education of the child—not to a particular group of children but to all the children in the world: the dance is the most natural and beautiful aid to the development of the growing child in its constant movement. And only that education is right which includes the dance.

When I founded my first school in 1905 I was only twenty-two years old. The basic reason for my putting in my whole capital, the first fruits of my success, and of sacrificing my personal career at that time, was a feeling of compassion for the misunderstanding and the torture that the average child goes through in the name of modern education. My primary reason for founding this school was not, as people seem to think, to train children for the theatre. Instead, while I myself was still almost a child, I was dreaming of educating and forming around me young disciples who would be inspired by my idea, living with me day by day and later helping to give to every child in the world the art that I had given them. For every child that is born in civilization has the right to a heritage of beauty.

My theories soon bore fruit. Within two years the school transformed insignificant, sickly and badly formed children into frescoes that outrivalled the loveliness of Donatello or Luca della Robbia. There is no more simple and direct means to give art to the people—to give a conception of art to the working man—than to transform his own children into living works of art. The children of my school at an early age learned to sing the chorals of Mendelssohn, Mozart, Bach and the songs of Schubert; for every child, no matter of what class, if he sings and moves to this music will penetrate the spiritual message of the great masters.

And so the first great aim of my school was social and educational. But I succeeded so well in giving this expression to the children that the bourgeois hailed them as phenomena, and were willing to pay large sums to put them on the stage and stare at them through opera glasses. How many times have I come out after a performance and explained: "These dancing children whom I have formed in my school are not performing as theatre artists. I bring them before you simply to show what can be accomplished with every child. Now give me the means to work this experiment in a greater field, and I will further prove that the beauty which you applaud to-night can be the natural expression of every child in the world."

But in order to carry out such a vast project it was necessary to have the supervision and aid of a government. Having appealed in vain to all the governments of Europe and America, I accepted an invitation from the Soviet Government to found a school in Moscow.

TERPSICHORE

What must we do to bring Terpsichore back amongst us again? We must recover: 1. the ideal beauty of the human form; and 2. the movement which is the expression of this form.

All my research and study in the field of the dance have been founded on these two principles.

Always the lines of a form truly beautiful suggest movement, even in repose. And always the lines that are truly beautiful in movement suggest repose, even in the swiftest flight. It is this quality of repose in movement that gives to movements their eternal element.

All movement on earth is governed by the law of gravitation, by attraction and repulsion, resistance and yielding; it is that which makes up the rhythm of the dance.

To discover this rhythm, we must listen to the pulsations of the earth. The great composers—Bach, Beethoven, Wagner—have in their works combined with absolute perfection terrestrial and human rhythm. And that is why I have taken as a guide the rhythms of the great Masters; not because I thought I could express the beauty of their works, but because, in surrendering my body unresistingly to their rhythms I have hoped to recover the natural cadences of human movements which have been lost for centuries.

There are documents wherein the two beauties are fixed in a perfect state—the ideal beauty of the human form and the ideal beauty of movement; these are the Greek vases collected in museums.

In the thousands and thousands of figures which I have studied on these vases, I have always found an undulating line as the point of departure. Every movement, even in repose, contains the quality of fecundity, possesses the power to give birth to another movement.

With the exception of some grotesque figures, or those dating from a poorer era, I have not found, for example, a single drawing in which the foot is raised to a line perpendicular to the body. Even on the vases with figures expressing Bacchic frenzy, this movement is unknown. That is because it expresses a "stop"; one knows that it cannot continue, that it can only be its own end.

On the other hand, in the leaping figures with bent knees, one senses that the movement goes on: there is in this movement an eternal element—one which follows the undulating line of the great forces of Nature, on which I have based all the movements of my dance. That is but one example, but one finds in thousands of figures the same principle.

One of the commonest figures in the Bacchic dances is that with the head turned backward. In this movement one senses immediately the Bacchic frenzy possessing the entire body. The motive underlying this gesture is in all nature. The animals, in Bacchic movement, turn back the head: in tropic countries, at night, the elephants turn their heads; dogs baying at the moon, lions, tigers. It is the universal Dionysiac movement. The waves of the ocean form this line under a storm, the trees in a tempest.

THE DANCE OF THE GREEKS

THE ONLY way to accomplish a re-birth of the dance is to restore it to its original place. To know the true place of the dance it is necessary to study history.

The oldest of the dances that were an art were those of Asia, and of Egypt—which influenced the Greek dance. But those earlier dances were not of our race; it is to Greece that we must turn, because all our dancing goes back to Greece. What, then, was the Greek dance?

For centuries before Aeschylus the people danced. They danced together and expressed thus their collective emotion, joyous, warlike, or sorrowing. It was out of this dance of the people that the Chorus developed, and the Chorus was the real beginning of tragedy.

There was later added to the Chorus the first *actor*. This actor recounted the incident, expressed the special feeling which the drama aroused in him; while the Chorus danced and sang as before, remaining on a plane above the drama.

Aeschylus added to this spectacle one or two actors. But the Chorus remained, for him, the soul of the tragedy. The actors represented only an incidental recital, details of the action, while the Chorus soared far above men's actions. Entering at the most poignant moment of emotional tension, it brought a lyric exaltation, the eternal and divine point of view. Deepest soul of Tragedy: the Chorus was Wisdom or Reason or Joy or Sorrow eternal.

But Sophocles, by increasing the number of actors lessened the rôle played by the Chorus. Euripides in turn increased the number of characters and thus further decreased the importance of the Chorus. Still, in the *Bacchae,* at the highest point touched in tragedy, it is still the Chorus which, with the God Dionysus, *is* the Bacchic expression; whereas the characters are not the intoxication itself but only beings under the influence of that intoxication, moved by an emotion of which they cannot attain the essence.

After Euripides the decadence came quickly. The value of the Chorus was no longer recognized. The end came in Rome, when the Chorus was replaced by mere *mimes*. They even undertook to mime *Oedipus!* Tragedy was dead.

Later, much later, efforts were made to revive tragedy: efforts admirable for the sincerity and the spirit of those who made them; but certain fundamental errors gave false direction to them, and made the realizations imperfect. The most serious of these errors was the failure to understand this truth: Tragedy is incomplete without the Chorus.

It was the ancient tragedy that Monteverde and other artists of his time wished to re-create. Monteverde had no intention of composing operas. "Opera" is a meaningless word. He intended to accomplish a renaissance of tragedy. But he made the error of giving the actors the task of expressing the soul of the music—a rôle reserved by the Greeks for the Chorus. This error was more firmly established by the followers of Monteverde. Thus the first steps in the Renaissance followed a path that led away from the true form of tragedy.

Glück, finally, revolted. One may say that he found again the Chorus. He made it sing. But the opposition he met with cramped his genius. He lived in an artificial and affected era. In tragedy he forgot the drama and the actor.

Richard Wagner re-found the drama, but he mistook the rôle of the Chorus; or at least he transferred it to the characters. The drama lives in the fortunes of the characters: it is the weaknesses or the grandeur in the soul of Oedipus, and what happens to him, that interests us. Drama develops out of the reactions of the characters toward each other and under the action of Fate. But Wagner thought to lift the characters above the drama, to give them the rôle of the Chorus. Thus in the second act of *Tristan and Isolde,* Brangäne, with her song that is too slow to be that of a protagonist in the drama, represents the Chorus. Tristan and Isolde, in their duet of love, become their own Chorus; because whenever two characters speak together even one word, they cease being the characters of the drama and become interpreters of the abstract, become the Chorus.

That brings us to modern times. We can understand now what we have lost and what we must find again.

How, today, shall we give back to the dance its original place? By identifying it again with the Chorus. It is necessary to give back the tragic Chorus to the dance, and to give back the dance to the other arts. The Chorus of tragedy is the true place of the dance. It is there that it must be, associated with tragedy and with the other arts. All the rest is decadence.

In the time of Sophocles dancing, poetry, music, dramaturgy and architecture formed one harmonious unity, as a single art manifested in different ways, truly one and the same thing. The association of tragic art and architecture was intimate, almost a fusion. All that went to complete a performance seemed shaped by the same law—that is, in the image of the ideal man or the man-god.

The characters and the Chorus, center of the drama, were the center of a harmonious ensemble, like the solar plexus at the center of the man. Toward them everything converged; from them everything went out like rays from a light.

Often at an hour when Athens was scarcely yet awake, I have danced in the Theatre of Dionysus. I have sensed how everything there was shaped in accordance with this same harmony. My place in the theatre was the center of the orchestra, and the gestures of my arms, before me, traced the lines following the natural horizon once formed by the top of the rings of seats. Today this harmony is destroyed.

The arts that were then grouped around tragedy have become separated. Architecture has turned aside: the builders of modern theatres have followed personal plans, obedient to the commercial idea, and have put up buildings inconvenient for both public and actors.

The dance thought that it could live separately, by itself—and it has arrived at that anomalous thing, the ballet. In either theatre or music hall the ballet is without true significance, without any accord with art. Even if all the world danced, the ballet still would be a false thing, for in the ballet the dance aspires to be everything, to take the place of poetry and drama.

The proof that the dance cannot exist alone is that it finds recourse to pantomime. The pantomimists pretend to speak with gestures; they try to imitate language. Art is more natural; it does not imitate, it does not seek out equivalents, it does not pretend to speak—it has its own language.

The Greek music is lost, so that the poetic text of the Choruses is no more than an indication out of which the harmony is lacking. In our own times we have no music created for the dance. It is thought that the dance is unworthy of beautiful music, and it is therefore deprived of it. The great geniuses of music alone have had rhythm in their work. That is why I have danced to the rhythms of Bach and of Glück, of Beethoven and of Chopin, of Schubert and of Wagner, because practically they alone have understood and have expressed the rhythm of the human body.

Wagner is the closest approach to a musician for the dance. But with him music absorbs everything. Certainly it is an offense artistically to dance to such music, but I have done it by necessity, because this music is awakening the dance that was dead, awakening rhythm. I have danced to it, driven by it as a leaf is driven before the wind.

After many years of study I have arrived at this conclusion: the natural rhythm of the human body and the rhythm of contemporary music are in complete disaccord; the simplest gesture fails to find in these notes a line which it can follow. But to the rhythm of the words of a Greek Chorus one dances easily. Just in hearing them one sees unfolding a frieze of sculptured figures in movement. The music of the Greeks must have accorded with the rhythms of these words. Ah, if it only could be recovered!

Today the theatre is divided into two halves, each ignoring and scornful of the other: the theatre of music and the theatre of the spoken word. Everything must be undone. The most beautiful dream is that of finding again the Greek theatre that is ideal for both spectators and actors. To bring to life again the ancient ideal! I do not mean to say, *copy* it, *imitate* it; but to *breathe its life, to recreate it in one's self, with personal inspiration:* to start from its beauty and then go toward the future. The subjects of the dramas can be modern. But to find again the ancient idea, and, by a miracle of love and devotion, to unite anew the arts and the artists!

To unite the arts around the Chorus, to give back to the dance its place as the Chorus, that is the ideal. When I have danced I have tried always to be the Chorus: I have been the Chorus of young girls hailing the return of the fleet, I have been the Chorus dancing the Pyrrhic Dance, or the Bacchic; I have never once danced a solo. The dance, again joined with poetry and with music, must become once more the tragic Chorus. That is its only and its true end. That is the only way for it to become again an art.

May the artists unite and accomplish this miracle of love!

DRAWING BY GRANDJOUAN SUGGESTED BY ISADORA DUNCAN

DANCING CÉSAR FRANCK'S REDEMPTION

© *L'Oeuvre, Paris*

DRAWING BY AUGUSTE RODIN

Reproduced from La Revue de L'Oeuvre

YOUTH AND THE DANCE

The child is gloriously full of life. He leaps endlessly, filled with the intoxication of movement. He is a young animal, growing in the midst of a joyous exaltation, drawing in with the intensity of all his being the forces for his future life.

The growing of the child, and all his movements, bear witness to a harmonious rhythm expressing all growing life. To "train" the child it is only necessary to understand that the surest road, and the most beautiful, is to surround his living with an atmosphere of graceful movement. From this early environment a deep love of beauty will naturally develop.

For an understanding of the dance, the activities of the child should be directed into the channels natural to the tastes and capacities of childhood. It is not necessary to ask of him great effort: let him breathe joyously, give free rein to his natural animation, having care only for the harmonious growth of his body. Above all do not force on him movements toward which his nature rebels, but only lead his spirit and his body into accord with the most noble movements and the most spiritual expressions of mankind. Then the body becomes a spirit whose gestures are its language, and the young soul opens out to light, beauty and everlasting love.

Let the child thrill to this quiet training, as to those artists whose human existence has ended but who have left an immortal music.

Let the child dance as a child: don't impose on him the attitudes and the gestures of an epoch which had nothing in common with simple living and true humanity—of the ballets of Louis XIV.

Let his dances express the soul of the child, at first in the beauty and the lack of self-consciousness that belong to babyhood, then in accord with youthfulness, then with adolescence. Don't teach young girls to imitate either nymphs or houris or courtesans, but make them dance like the vestals of ancient times, who consecrated themselves two thousand years ago.

Conserve to the adolescents their strength and their full-lived youth. Do not dress them in fantastic costumes, which make them look like clowns or languishing lovers. Rather let their dance be the reflection of the eternal ideal of glorious youth—youth's dreams and aspirations made living. Let their dance be born of joyousness and strength and courage. Let it breathe the holy spirit of sacrifice of the young soldier!

And when they become embodiments of the modern vestals, they will be transformed: women in love with love and with the joy of motherhood. At this moment their dance, completed and distinctive, will be the most beautiful of all.

Yes, let us admire the natural dance of the young women and the young men, their transformation, under their pulsating rhythm—in their dance that is perfect and complete, containing all life and bringing the dancers close to the gods. The crowd will follow their steps, will watch their attitudes, becoming one with them in a perfect harmony, combining, on their side, the most noble expression of human life and the clear call of divinity.

When that day dawns, that day of final happiness, we shall know the fulfillment of the sublime rhythms of Beethoven's Symphonies.

DEPTH

THE TRUE dance is an expression of serenity; it is controlled by the profound rhythm of inner emotion. Emotion does not reach the moment of frenzy out of a spurt of action; it broods first, it sleeps like the life in the seed, and it unfolds with a gentle slowness. The Greeks understood the continuing beauty of a movement that mounted, that spread, that ended with a promise of re-birth. The Dance—it is the rhythm of all that dies in order to live again; it is the eternal rising of the sun.

It is not for us to arrive at knowledge; we know, as we love, by instinct, faith, emotion.

Emotion works like a motor. It must be warmed up to run well, and the heat does not develop immediately; it is progressive. The dance follows the same law of development, of progression. The true dancer, like every true artist, stands before Beauty in a state of complete suspense; he opens the way to his soul and his "genius," and he lets himself be swayed by them as the trees abandon themselves to the winds. He starts with one slow movement and mounts from that gradually, following the rising curve of his inspiration, up to those gestures that exteriorize his fullness of feeling, spreading ever wider the impulse that has swayed him, fixing it in another expression.

The movements should follow the rhythm of the waves: the rhythm that rises, penetrates, holding in itself the impulse and the after-movement; call and response, bound endlessly in one cadence.

Our modern dances know nothing of this first law of harmony. Their movements are choppy, end-stopped, abrupt. They lack the continuing beauty of the curve. They are satisfied with being the points of angles which spur on the nerves. The music of today, too, only makes the nerves dance. Deep emotion, spiritual gravity, are entirely lacking. We dance with the jerky gestures of puppets. We do not know how to get down to the depths, to lose ourselves in an inner self, how to develop our visions into the harmonies that attend our dreams.

We are always in paroxysms. We walk angularly. We strain ourselves always to hold a balance between points. We are ignorant of the repose of a descent, and the comfort of breathing, of mounting again, skimming, returning, like a bird, to rest. The bird never struggles. The dancer ought to be light as a flame. Even violence is the greater when it is restrained: one gesture that has grown slowly out of that reserve is worth many thousands that struggle and cut each other off.

THE GREAT SOURCE

THERE was a time when I filled many notebooks with notes and observations, when I burned with apostolic fire for my art, and gave myself up to deep convictions and naive daring. At that time I wanted to make over human life, down to its least details of costume, of morals, of way of living. But that was ten years ago. I have had, since, the leisure to discover the vanity of those noble ambitions, and I am satisfied now with the joys of my work, preoccupied by my art itself.

One explains the dance better by dancing than by publishing commentaries and treatises. An art should be able to do without all that, moreover; its truth will blaze forth spontaneously if it is really beautiful.

And so, I do not wish to spin theories or put down a set of principles. But I may perhaps say, without being accused of preaching, what has always been my underlying thought about the dance.

For me the dance is not only the art that gives expression to the human soul through movement, but also the foundation of a complete conception of life, more free, more harmonious, more natural. It is not, as is too generally believed, a composition of steps, arbitrary and growing out of mechanical combinations—which even if they serve well as technical exercises cannot pretend that they constitute an art. This is the means, not the end.

I have studied thoroughly the represented figures of all ages and of all the great master-artists, and I have never yet seen one shown walking on the points of the toes or raising the leg to the height of the head. These ugly and false positions do not at all express that state of Dionysiac abandon which the dancer must know. True movements, moreover, are not invented; they are discovered—just as in music one does not invent harmonies but only discovers them.

The great and the only principle on which I feel myself justified in leaning, is a constant, absolute and universal unity between form and movement; a rhythmic unity which runs through all the manifestations of Nature. The waters, the winds, the plants, living creatures, the particles of matter itself obey this controlling rhythm of which the characteristic line is the wave. In nothing does Nature suggest jumps and breaks; there is between all the conditions of life a continuity or flow which the dancer must respect in his art, or else become a mannequin—outside Nature and without true beauty.

To seek in Nature the most beautiful forms and to discover the movement which expresses the soul of those forms, that is the task of the dancer. Like the sculptor, with whom he has so much in common, the dancer should draw his inspiration from Nature alone. Rodin wrote: "In sculpture it is not necessary to copy the works of antiquity. One must rather observe the works of Nature first, and then see in the works of the ancient sculptors only the way in which Nature has been interpreted."

Rodin is right; and in my art I have not at all copied, as is believed, figures from Greek vases, friezes or paintings. I have learned from them how to study Nature, and when certain of my movements recall gestures seen on the works of art, it is only because they likewise are taken from the great natural source.

I am inspired by the movement of the trees, the waves, the snows, by the connection between passion and the storm, between the breeze and gentleness, and so on. And I always put into my movements a little of that divine continuity which gives to all of Nature its beauty and life.

That is not saying that it is enough just to wave the arms and legs, in order to have a natural dance. In art the simplest works are those which have cost the most in the effort for synthesis, of observation and of creation; and all the greatest masters know what is the cost of true accord with the great and unrivalled model that is Nature.

Since I was a child I have spent twenty years of incessant labor in the service of my art, a large part of that time being devoted to technical training—which I am sometimes accused of lacking. That is because, I repeat, technique is not an end but only a means.

The dance, in my opinion, has for its purpose the expression of the most noble and the most profound feelings of the human soul: those which rise from the gods in us, Apollo, Pan, Bacchus, Aphrodite. The dance must implant in our lives a harmony that is glowing and pulsing. To see in the dance only a frivolous or pleasant diversion is to degrade it.

There are continual reactions of the body and the spirit which the ancients did not neglect, but which we too often have misunderstood. Plato danced, as did the magistrates and the officers in the ancient republics; this custom gave to their thoughts a grace and a balance which have immortalized them. That is only natural: the attitude we assume affects our soul; a simple turning backward of the head, made with passion, sends a Bacchic frenzy running through us, of joy or heroism or desire. All gestures thus give rise to an inner response, and similarly they have the power to express directly every possible state of the feelings or thought.

Every movement that can be danced on the seashore, without being in harmony with the rhythm of the waves, every movement that can be danced in the forest without being in harmony with the swaying of the branches, every movement that one can dance nude, in the sunshine, in the open country, without being in harmony with the life and the solitude of the landscape—every such movement is false, in that it is out of tune in the midst of Nature's harmonious lines. That is why the dancer should above all else choose movements that express the strength, health, nobility, ease and serenity of living things.

© *L'Oeuvre, Paris*

DRAWING BY AUGUSTE RODIN

Reproduced from La Revue de L'Oeuvre

© *L'Oeuvre, Paris*

DRAWING BY AUGUSTE RODIN

Reproduced from La Revue de L'Oeuvre

RICHARD WAGNER

It seems to me that the compositions of Wagner cannot be considered as the work of one artist or as the expression of one country. They are rather the entire revolt and all the feeling of an epoch, expressed through the medium of Richard Wagner.

That is why it seems so petty to have wished to abandon this music during the war; for the work of Wagner flows through every drop of blood in every artist of the world, and his mighty rhythm has become part of every heart-beat of each one of us. For Wagner is more than an artist: he is the glorious far-seeing prophet, liberator of the art of the future. It is he who will give birth to the new union of the arts, the rebirth of the theatre, tragedy and the dance as one.

He was the first to conceive of the dance as born of music. This is my conception of the dance also, and for it I strive in the work of my school. For in the depths of every musical theme of Wagner, dances will be found: monumental sculpture, movement which only demands release and life.

It is of this music that critics are wont to say, "It is not written for the dance"; but it is from this music that the dance, so long lifeless in the embryo, is being born again. In comparison with this new-born dance, the posed attitudes of the dancers of the Opera appear to us like the figures in the wax-works museums.

The theatre will live again in all its glory only when the dance once more takes its true place, as an integral and inevitable part of tragedy. It is because I believe this that I have dared to dance to the music of Wagner—yes, that I have raised my hands, vibrant with ecstasy, to the harmonious chords of *Parsifal*.

Do you understand the gigantic task that is imposed on us, before we can wrench from this music the torrential movement that must come—the glorious child-birth of the Dance?

1921.

A LETTER TO THE PUPILS

Please don't let any one persuade you to try to dance to Debussy. It is only the music of the *Senses* and has no message to the Spirit. And then the gesture of Debussy is all *inward*—and has no outward or upward. I want you to dance only that music which goes from the soul in mounting circles. Why not study the *Suite in Re* of Bach? Do you remember my dancing it? Please also continue always your studies of the Beethoven Seventh and the Schubert Seventh, and why not dance with Copeland the seven Minuets of Beethoven that we studied in Fourth Avenue? And the Symphony in G of Mozart. And there is a whole world of Mozart that you might study.

Plunge your soul in divine unconscious *Giving* deep within it, until it gives to your soul its *Secret*. That is how I have always tried to express music. My soul should become one with it, and the dance born from that embrace. Music has been in all my life the great Inspiration and will be perhaps some day the Consolation, for I have gone through such terrible years. No one has understood since I lost Deirdre and Patrick how pain has caused me at times to live almost in a delirium. In fact my poor brain has more often been crazed than any one can know. Sometimes quite recently I feel as if I were awakening from a long fever. When you think of these years, think of the Funeral March of Schubert, the *Ave Maria,* the *Redemption,* and forget the times when my poor distracted soul trying to escape from suffering may well have given you all the appearance of madness.

I have reached such high peaks flooded with light, but my soul had no strength to live there—and no one has realized the horrible torture from which I have tried to escape. Some day if you understand sorrow you will understand too all I have lived through, and then you will only think of the light towards which I have pointed and you will know the *real* Isadora is there. In the meantime work and create Beauty and Harmony. The poor world has need of it, and with your six spirits going with one will, you can create Beauty and Inspiration for a new Life.

I am so happy that you are working and that you love it. Nourish your spirits from Plato and Dante, from Goethe and Schiller, Shakespeare and Nietzsche (don't forget that the *Birth of Tragedy* and the *Spirit of Music* are my Bible), and with these to guide you, and the greatest music, you may go far.

Dear children, I take you all in my arms. And here is a kiss for Anna, and here one for Therese, and one for Irma, and here is a kiss for Gretel and one for little Erika—and a kiss for you, dearest Lisel. Let us pray that this separation will only bring us nearer and closer in a higher communion—and soon we will all dance together a *Reigen*. All my love.

MOSCOW IMPRESSIONS

(These letters about her attempt to found a school of the dance under the Communist State in Russia are grouped to indicate I. D.'s enthusiasm, her planning, her methods of teaching, and the final discouragements she met. The first is an open letter to the English press; it exists in her own handwriting—so that no one need be tempted to think that it was put out by the Soviet publicity offices. The second is unaddressed; the third a letter in French beginning *Cher Camarade;* the fourth to Augustin Duncan; the others apparently to Soviet officials.)

This coming to Russia is a tremendous experience, and I would not have missed it for anything. Here at last is a frame mighty enough to work in, and for the first time in my life I feel that I can stretch out my arms and breathe. Here one feels that perhaps for the second time in the world's history a great force has arisen to give capitalism, which stands for monstrous greed and villainy, one great blow. The dragon, man-eating, labor exploiting, has here received his death stroke. What matters it that in his final throes he has cast destruction about him? The valiant hero who smote him still lives, though enfeebled from the deadly struggle, and from him will be born a new world.

A new world, a newly created mankind; the destruction of the old world of class injustice, and the creation of the new world of equal opportunity. That is the work one is viewing here, and for this work it fills my soul with joy and pride that I am called upon to assist in its first steps, in the teaching of the children. A great school of new beings who will be worthy the ideals of the new world. A community of boys and girls to live in a great school, to form the future men and maidens who will be the upholders of Communism—future idealists.

Relegated to the past is the old ideal of youth, with its limited prize of monogamistic love and its narrow ideal of family life as the goal of existence. The future love will be not "my family" but "all humanity," not "my children" but "all children," not "my country" but "all peoples."

I salute the birth of the future community of International love.

Moscow is certainly one of the most interesting if not the most interesting center of the world today. Yes, despite the hardship and suffering, here is a source. I would rather be here today than in any so-called prosperous city, and the suffering I observe seems to me at least a more beautiful expression than the new-rich and the munition-proprietors, smug and overfed, riding about in automobiles in search of pleasure, which they seldom find. Let them come here to feed the Volga district—they might find happiness by reflection.

I predict that Moscow will soon be the most sought out city, a sort of spiritual Klondike. Tired artists, idealists, searchers after truth, will all be flocking here to this great well-spring of spiritual enlightenment for mankind. For my part, that art with which I was born and which I know all the children of the world are in need of, I hope to give here, to these children who are suffering from the want of all material things. I will give them this great Spiritual treasure of my art, not served up in copies and caricatures that have been made of it, paralysed by theories and killed by systems—Dalcroze and others—but this art spontaneous and true, as God gave it to me, as Walt Whitman said, "for reasons."

The magnificent idea of giving music for the people—are we going to see that dropped? I have seen the people here listening to music only in the churches, and there the music is very beautiful, but mixed with such a large portion of shallow superstition that it is more harmful than good. Why not have a great theatre where the people can enter freely, as in a church, without tickets, at least on Sunday afternoons and evenings; where one could give successively the symphonies of Beethoven, the music of Wagner, Bach, Schubert, etc., and where all the children can dance?

I am hard at work here at present, all day, selecting talented children from the hundreds and hundreds that apply. It looks as if all the children in Russia wanted to come to this school, and it is very touching to see the eagerness of these children, and their desire to learn something beautiful. I think that at last we have the promised school. I am giving a performance on the 7th of November, at the Grand Opera House, for an audience of Communists: Tchaikowsky's Sixth Symphony and *Marche Slav*. Conditions have changed here; all places in the theatres are now paid for. Mine will be the only performance that is given this winter free for the people. I have been here three months; we have already a school with two studios, a rose-colored one and a blue one—the curtains of which I brought from Paris. We have beds for a hundred children, and in the neighborhood a great *salle* where I will teach five hundred children each day. . . .

The streets of Moscow are the picture of the song of the "Open Road" of Walt Whitman. He was the first Bolshevik. I am never tired of the crowds in the streets. A painter would find great opportunities here—life and color on a big scale. Steichen would be wild with joy. You should tell him to come here. . . .

The theatre life in Moscow is most progressive and intense. There are two or three Art theatres, with such futuristic ideas that Stanislavsky seems quite old-fashioned, but he is still the greatest artist of all. Thursday night we saw Oscar Wilde's *Salome* in the Kamerny

Theatre, where they believe that every actor should be dancer, singer, pantomimist. They have a symphony orchestra, and dance, sing, declaim, all in one. The effect is somewhat Chinese, only without the Chinese imagination. Fine color, form, wonderful light effects, some beautiful bodies; the only criticism I could make is a lack of subtlety and imagination, and everything coming more from the outside than within. Also a contradiction between symbolic gesture and at other moments a complete realism—as when Salome wipes the floor with the head of John the Baptist. I decided that they did not quite know whether they were symbolists or realists, but I admired the tremendous amount of work and care they evidently put into it. It is a wonderful architectural theatre, built on the same scale as Bayreuth. . . . But I do not approve of the custom here of non-applauding public; it makes too great a division between the actors and public. I think, on the contrary, one should work toward a theatre in which the public would take part more and more in the performance, even in eventual responses, singing of choruses, etc. The public here seems quite dead, and in the different concerts I have gone to, I look in vain for the great enthusiastic public of before the war. Enthusiasm of the public is necessary to give life to the artist. . . .

We have already six American pupils, three English and two French, so you see the school is international.

This summer the children of my school who have lived and studied here for three years, under the most difficult circumstances, enduring cheerfully a life of hardship, held a meeting together and decided that in spite of the fact that they had no material wealth of any sort, they felt the need to give their art to others. They decided that they would call a meeting of a thousand children of workers and teach them the Art which had given themselves a new life of beauty.

A meeting took place in the Great Sports Ground of the Red

Stadium, at whose head is the Comrade Podvoisky. With the help of Comrade Podvoisky classes were organized and every afternoon of the last three months of this summer our brave little class of forty have taught hundreds of children to dance.

Children who came to the first meeting pale and weak, who could at first hardly walk or skip or raise their arms to the sky, have become transformed under the influence of the air, the sunshine, the music and the joy of dancing taught them by our young pioneers. Their costume is a simple tunic without sleeves and reaching only to the knees.

Movement is a language as powerful and expressive as words. I could not explain my lessons in words to these children, but I spoke to them by the language of movements, and they, by their responsive movement, showed me that they understood.

"Children, place your hands here, as I do, on your breast, feel the life within you; this movement means MAN—and the children answered in chorus, *'Chelovek'*; and now, raise the arms slowly upwards and outwards towards the heavens, this movement means UNIVERSE;—the children chorused, *'Vselennaya.'* Let your hands fall slowly downwards to the EARTH—and the chorus responded *'Zemlia.'* Now, stretch your hands towards me in love, this means COMRADE—chorus, *'Tovarisch.'*"

I watched these hundreds of children dancing. Sometimes they resembled a field of red poppies swaying in the wind, at other times, seeing them rushing forward together, one perceived that they were a horde of young warriors and Amazons, ready to do battle for the ideals of the New World.

But the best of all was the enthusiasm and happiness of the children themselves—how they loved to throw themselves heart and soul into beautiful movement; and when song was added to the dancing, it seemed that their entire being was lifted in exaltation of the complete and joyous rhythms of youth.

I would respectfully call to your notice that my school is the only artistic effort formed during Communism that has constantly, through me and through my pupils, awakened in all the towns of Russia the heartfelt, genuine enthusiasm of the Workers, of their wives and of their children. I danced alone, and afterwards with my pupils, for the miners in Baku in their own theatres and for their children; for Communists throughout all the theatres of Russia, and for the children of Lenn Staat outside of Kief, not once but many times, gratuitously; and during that time I was paying my own expenses from my private bank account, drawn from the sale of my property in France.

I was forced to leave this School from lack of any support whatever from the Soviet Government, while I saw other schools that had raised no enthusiasm among the workers and whose tendencies were frankly unhealthy and decadent, supported by the same Government that had refused me aid for my work.

When the children of my School danced before the Workers, they arose and shouted with joy, and why? Because they themselves were the children of workers and because I had taught them to express, in simple and natural movements, the heroic struggles and ideals which were nascent in their blood. Therefore every worker could understand their Art, and the proof is that my school, now dancing in China, is at once understood and acclaimed by the Chinese workers. They have expressed a wish to have this dancing taught to their children.

The letter about this is the first word I have heard from the school for *six months,* and the first knowledge I have had that they are in China. I wish to protest that this School which I formed at the sacrifice of my fortune and person, and for which I had become naturally boycotted by all my former friends and audiences in Europe, should be allowed to pass from my control and into the hands of private speculation. Those sacrifices that I made, I made gladly for the cause of the people; but when it comes to the exploitation of my work by private organization without so much as asking my advice—I must protest! This is an exploitation of my art which I would not have expected, considering the primary object of my visit to Russia was to escape from just such exploitation of Art, which Soviet Russia condemned Europe for in 1921.

The Camerade Lunacharsky wrote of my school:

"Isadora Duncan wanted to give a natural and beautiful education to every child. The Bourgeois society, however, did not understand this and put her pupils on the stage to exploit them for money. We will know how to act differently."

I ask *when?*

1921-1927.

REFLECTIONS, AFTER MOSCOW

You ask me to give my impressions of Soviet Russia. You will readily understand that not all the people living in Russia see alike the events there taking place. The avowed Communists, those who go to the extreme of wanting to see equal opportunity and happiness for all, actually do see the door open to the workers of the future; whereas the bourgeois, having in the past lived in a selfish security and comfort, can see and only want to see in these same changes what they call "the end of Russia."

Always great artists have had this dream: to create their art for all humanity, for the people. Unfortunately, for those of our time this dream cannot become reality, because in every country where it might be realized, they have before them always the same public—that which is able to pay the demanded price for good seats. All the students and the poorer people—those whose spirit urges them toward the beautiful—are deprived almost entirely of the artist's work; or else, if occasionally they do enjoy it, they are obliged to sit in "nigger heaven," where usually the acoustics are very bad and the view of the stage distorted.

I have always worried over this condition. That is why, hoping to see my dream finally become reality, I turned toward Russia, when the Soviet Government announced that it was going to open the theatre to all the people.

In 1905 in Berlin I had already tried the experiment of giving

Courtesy Musée Rodin, Paris

DRAWING BY AUGUSTE RODIN

SKETCHES OF ISADORA DUNCAN DANCING, BY MAURICE DENIS

recitals for the workingmen. These occasions had been quite successful. I had found among those simple people a touching appreciation, which proved that I had brought into their lives a fresh experience of light and beauty.

It was then that I founded in Berlin a school, free to the children of working people. My plan was to develop a small group who would later become the teachers of the boys and girls of the working class.

No government recognized the value of my school, or the beauty of my idea. Even my pupils after a while were so transformed by the training I gave them that they came to consider themselves talented artists, so that they forgot their mission and left the group, to follow impresarios who were ready to exploit them and to take them on recital tours through all the world.

After fifteen years of work and care, I found that I must begin my task all over again. One young girl only was faithful to me, preferring to be true to the trust I had put in her. She followed me to Moscow, where she is now, directing my workers' school.

People have never understood my true aim. They have thought that I wished to form a troupe of dancers to perform in the theatre. Certainly nothing was farther from my thoughts. Far from wishing to develop theatre dancers, I have only hoped to train in my school numbers of children who through dance, music, poetry and song would express the feelings of the people, with grace and beauty.

Alas! It took only too short a time to learn that I could not carry out this work unaided; I must find a government enlightened enough to support it. I went successively to America, to France, to England, to Greece—and no one of these countries would give me aid. It was only natural that I should turn to the Soviets, when they announced the plan of making the theatre free to all. Was not that my only way, my unique opportunity to bring my school into existence?

In 1921 I believed that my dream had actually taken form, for on arriving in Moscow I found the theatres really open to all, and filled with workers at every performance. On my part, I gave several recitals before thousands of poor people. I had the joy of absolute expression. For the first time in my artistic career, it seemed to me that the horizon was widened.

This hope did not last long, since in 1922, with the change in political control, all the artists' dreams of giving art without charge to the workers faded away. The theatre became again a commercial enterprise. While the concerts had been free, many artists complained that the workers did not understand the works of Beethoven, and that not understanding them they were incapable of listening to them quietly. This was caused entirely by the too abrupt change from a life of hard labor to the highest summits of art. To develop the taste of the working people, it is necessary to begin at the beginning—that is, with the children.

The children of my school, four or five years old, in learning to move in harmony with the rhythms of Schubert or of Mozart, or in the minuets of Beethoven, acquire gradually and without effort a taste for this music; and with natural instinct they learn to discern the difference between superior music and poor music.

They are taken often, moreover, to visit the museums, and helped by explanations they understand very quickly the nobility of Egyptian, Greek or modern sculpture. Invariably, upon their return to the school, they try to re-create the different movements of the sculptured figures, and often they find something very beautiful in this way. Thanks to this daily training, the humble children of the workers become themselves works of art which their parents can understand, and through whom they may come to know and to love what is beauty and grace—in a word, the experience of art.

Education of the young is the only way to bring taste and understanding to the working class. It is one of the great truths that what it is impossible to teach the child through words will be learned easily through the language of movement. The pedagogues have rarely understood the necessity of training the body of the child. German and Swedish gymnastics have in view only the development of the muscles; they neglect the proper correlation of spirit and body. I have taken as a foundation for my teaching that a child should never be given a movement that would not at the same time be an expression of the soul. A child ought to dance as naturally as a plant grows. An inner force ought to come to the surface and find expression. But in modern gymnastics it is the other way round: a force from the outside directs the movements under control of the will. Every animal in nature moves in harmony with the universal rhythm. It is only the child of man that finds itself controlled by unnatural movements.

Since the founding of my school in 1905, there have been formed, all over the world, thousands of schools which have copied—or thought they copied—my system. They all have made one fundamental mistake: I have no system. My only purpose and my only effort have been to lead the child each day to grow and to move according to an inner impulse; that is, in accordance with Nature. But all these schools have made the same mistake of dissecting the child's movements, and laying them out in geometric patterns, instead of letting all the natural grace and loveliness come to expression.

No art antique or modern has been able to reveal all that man can be when inspired by his highest aspirations, in terms of movement. William Blake alone has given an indication of it. Nietzsche had a vision of it, for he called on all humanity in the strophes of Beethoven's Fifth Symphony. Nevertheless, this vision is not impossible to realize, for I have seen the little children of my school, under the spell of music, drop all materiality and move with a beauty so pure that they attained the highest expression of human living. But to attain that height, the dance cannot be thought of as an amusement or as an exhibition on a stage before an audience avid of sensations. Until that day when the dance becomes the expression and the perfection of the crowd, it will be only a sort of gymnastic, a revelation of mediocrity.

At Moscow I worked during a whole summer with hundreds of workers' children. Their lessons were given in the open air. At the end of the season the results of the course were truly marvelous. From all parts of the city people came to see the children dance and sing. Alas, when winter came I was obliged to abandon the work, having no studio large enough, and above all having no way of providing adequate heat. It was sad to see the disappointment and despair of the children who had commenced to live a new and finer life in their dancing. Still, that which I did for Russia I am ready to begin doing again, for any other country whose government will give me the necessary aid.

The day is coming when a grand international school of children, where there will be a fairer conception of life, will open the doors of the future to a new humanity. This school that I have wanted to found for twenty years, I hope for with a confidence ever increasing.

1927.

DANCING IN RELATION TO RELIGION AND LOVE

SINCE the earliest days of man's civilization, since the first temple that he constructed, there has always been a God, a central figure in the temple. The pose of this God is also an expression of his being and might be called a dance.

In 1899 I first saw Eleonora Duse in London, playing in a third-rate play called *The Second Mrs. Tanqueray*. The play goes through two acts of utter vulgarity and banality and I was shocked to see the divine Duse lending herself to such commonplace characterization. At the end of the third act, where Mrs. Tanqueray is driven to the wall by her enemies and, overcome with ennui, resolves to commit suicide, there was a moment when the Duse stood quite still, alone on the stage. Suddenly, without any special outward movement, she seemed to grow and grow until her head appeared to touch the roof of the theatre, like the moment when Demeter appeared before the house of Metaneira and disclosed herself as a Goddess. In that supreme gesture Duse was no longer the second Mrs. Tanqueray, but some wonderful goddess of all ages, and her growth before the eyes of the audience into that divine presence was one of the greatest artistic achievements I have ever witnessed. I remember that I went home dazed with the wonder of it. I said to myself, when I can come on the stage and stand as still as Eleonora Duse did tonight, and, at the same time, create that tremendous force of dynamic movement, then I shall be the greatest dancer in the world. At that point in *The Second Mrs. Tanqueray*,

Duse's spirit rose to such exalted heights that she became a part of the movement of the spheres. This is the highest expression of religion in the dance: that a human being should no longer seem human but become transmuted into the movements of the stars.

In 100 A. D. there stood on one of the hills of Rome a school which was known as the Seminary of Dancing Priests of Rome. The boys were chosen from the most aristocratic families. More than that, they had to possess lineage which dated back many hundreds of years and upon which no stain had ever fallen. Although they were taught all the arts and philosophies, dancing was their chief expression. They would dance in the theatre at the four different seasons of the year, Spring, Summer, Autumn and Winter. On these occasions they descended from their hill to Rome, where they took part in ceremonies and danced before the people for the purification of those who beheld them. These boys danced with such happy ardor and such purity that their dance influenced and elevated their audience, acting like medicine upon sick souls. It is of such expression that I have dreamed.

It must always be kept in mind that there are two classes of dancing: the sacred and the profane. By profane, I do not mean sinful, but simply that dancing which expresses the physical being and the joy of the senses, whereas sacred dancing expresses the aspirations of the spirit to transform itself into a higher sphere than the terrestrial. Very little is known in our day of the magic which resides in movement, and the potency of certain gestures. The number of physical movements that most people make through life is extremely limited. Having stifled and disciplined their movements in the first states of childhood, they resort to a set of habits seldom varied. So, too, their mental activities respond to set formulas, often repeated. With this repetition of physical and mental movements, they limit their expression until they become like actors who each night play the same role. With these few stereotyped

SKETCHES OF ISADORA DUNCAN DANCING, BY MAURICE DENIS

DRAWING BY JOSÉ CLARÁ

gestures, their whole lives are passed without once suspecting the world of the dance which they are missing.

Nietzsche said, "Let that day be called lost on which I have not danced." The entire *Zarathustra* is filled with phrases about man in his dancing being.

I have always deplored the fact that I was forced to dance in a theatre where people paid for their seats; a theatre with its stupid box-like stage handed down from the days of the Italian Guignol; and where the spectators' attitude is that of people who sit still and look but do not participate. Of course, in moments of great enthusiasm when the audience arises and applauds, they manifest a degree of dance participation. But I have dreamed of a more complete dance expression on the part of the audience, at a theatre in the form of an amphitheatre, where there would be no reason why, at certain times, the public should not arise and, by different gestures of dance, participate in my invocation. Something of this must have existed in the ancient cults of Apollo and Dionysus. Something of this still exists in the rituals of the Catholic church and also in the Greek church, where the congregation alternately rises, kneels and bows, in response to the invocations of the priest. I had always hoped that the day would come when we could have such a temple where the public, participating in different ways with me in my dance, would arrive at a much fuller enjoyment than they ever will experience by simply sitting as spectators.

Scriabine, the Russian composer, whose premature death saddened the musical world, was one of the world's greatest poets and geniuses. He not only was a great composer, but had the vision of complete musical expression in form, color and movement. When I had the joy of meeting him in Moscow in 1912 and telling him my ideas for a school and temple, he told me that the ideal of his life was to build such a temple in India, where at the same time, with full orchestral harmonies, the audience would be bathed in colors. His ideas were so in accord with my visions that we confidently looked forward to going to India together and participating in the creation of this temple. Alas, the war and his early death cut this short. I do not know whether Scriabine has ever written anything definite about his plans for uniting color, light and movement in an apotheosis of beauty, but I am convinced that one day his genius will find its expression through some medium.

In childhood we feel the religious sense of movement poignantly, for the mind is not yet clouded with dogmas or creeds. Children give themselves up entirely to the celebration and worship of the unknown God, "Whatever gods may be." In fact a child can understand many things through the movement of its body which would be impossible for it to comprehend by the medium of the written or spoken word. Many profound secrets of the outer and inner meanings of Nature and natural forces can be given to the child through the dance. One of the first to understand this was Jean-Jacques Rousseau, who in his book *Émile, or the Education of the Child,* even went so far as to say that a child should not be taught to read or write until its twelfth year. Up to that time all of its knowledge should be gained through music and dancing. It is curious that although this, one of the greatest discourses upon the education of the child, was written over a hundred years ago, the most modern schools have not awakened to it yet and still torment the bodies of children, vainly striving to appeal to their immature intelligence through the medium of words which mean very little to children.

I have often had an example of this in teaching a child the meaning of a poem. A simple poem which I thought any child would understand, the child would learn by heart, but when I would question it on the meaning of the different verses, the response would be a jumble of words of which it was incapable of comprehending the real significance. Then I would take the same poem and teach the child to dance it in gesture and emotional translation of movement, and I would have the pleasure of seeing the face of the child light up with understanding, and would know that he had actually learned through the movement of this poem what he was quite incapable of understanding from the words.

People have an entirely false conception of the importance of words in comparison with other modes of expression, just as potent as words. An entire audience of so called respectable people, who would leave the theatre if anyone appeared to blaspheme or to use indecent words, will sit through a performance in which someone makes indecent movements which, if translated into words, would make the audience rush from the theatre. A seemingly modest young girl would not think of addressing a young man in lines or spoken phrases which were indecent and yet the same girl will arise and dance these phrases with him in such dances as the Charleston and Black Bottom, while a negro orchestra is playing *Shake that thing!*

It is because of this that theatre censors have descended upon plays in New York and threatened to put their casts in jail for immoral propaganda, while in the music hall next door the movements of the dancers, if put into words, would be of such filth and immorality that it would be closed at once by the police. This is true because people have not learned that the expression of movement and of musical sounds is quite as clear to those who understand it as words are. To anyone who is as sensitive to movements as I am, nine-tenths of the movements that are made in the ordinary drawing room would be shocking, not because of their indecency but because of their indecent sterility. Therefore, I condemn the modern dances not so much for the indecency of their expression as because they are essentially sterile and futile. Young people who practice them for any length of time generally become as futile and frivolous as the movements they have been practicing, just as their minds would become if they were fed continually on a diet of penny novels and bad poems. I say it is of the utmost importance to a nation to train its children to the understanding and execution of movements of great heroic and spiritual beauty; to raise their many bans on the realization of sex, which is a fine thing in itself, and to put these same prohibitions on the frivolous caricatures and symbols of sex which are found in such dances as the fox trot and Black Bottom.

If, twenty years ago, when I first pleaded with America to adopt my school and my theories of dancing in all the public schools, they had acceded to my request, this deplorable modern dancing, which has its roots in the ceremonies of African primitives, could never have become dominant. It is extraordinary that mothers who would be intensely shocked if their daughters should indulge in a real orgy (which, after all, might not be so hurtful to them—since a real orgy might, like a real storm, clear the atmosphere for purer things)—these mothers will look on with smiling complacency at their daughters indulging in licentious contortions upon a dance floor, before their very eyes.

When I was fifteen years old and I realized that there was no teacher in the world who could give me any help in my desire to be a dancer, because at that time the only school that existed was the ballet, I turned, as I had noticed all other artists except dancers do, to the study of nature. Is anything more marvellous or beautiful in nature than the study of the delicate love movements of plants? My imagination was first captured by Shelley's wonderful poem *The Sensitive Plant,* and for my dances I studied the movements of the opening of flowers, and the flight of bees and the charming graces of pigeons and other birds. All of these seemed to be expressions of nature and of the love dance that runs through all life. I had read of the dance of the elephants in the moonlight and the dinosauric lifting of their trunks. The sudden reversal of the heads of the lions and tigers came to be associated in my mind with the tossing of the heads of the Bacchante.

These are the noblest love motions in Nature, just as the wriggling from the waist downwards of such dancing as the Charleston is the most ignoble. In the practicing of the dance in its relation to love, we should practice those movements which are ennobling rather than those which defile the divine image of the naked human being. Often when people have questioned my morals, I have answered that I consider myself extremely moral because in all my relations I have only made movements which seem beautiful to me.

In the old Greek myths there was always the transformation of the god into some element to express his love-making. Zeus appeared to Semele as the lightning; to Danae in the form of a golden mist; to Europa in the form of a bull; to Leda as a white swan. These are really only symbols of the beautiful form and movement of all love. This is the real dance of love—that element which takes on all parts of nature and becomes, in turn, a cloud, a mist, a fire, a bull or a white swan. All lovers who glory in the real beauty of love know these forms. And what a mockery that it should have come about in our epoch that one of the most beautiful expressions of Bacchic and sensuous love that has ever been written (I refer to the Bacchanal of Wagner's *Tannhäuser*) should be portrayed by three ballet dancers, in stiff skirts, standing on the tips of their toes in pink ballet slippers! I saw this when I arrived in Bayreuth in 1905.

People ask me, do you consider love-making an art and I would answer that not only love but every part of life should be practiced as an art. For we are no longer in the state of the primitive savage, but the whole expression of our life must be created through culture and the transformation of intuition and instinct into art.

1927.

FRAGMENTS AND THOUGHTS

I speak to you this afternoon as an egotist and a person of one idea, an idea to which I have devoted my entire life, which I have so lived, so loved, so thought of, that I may be able to interpret its interest and beauty to you.

I asked the Hon. C. D. [Chauncey Depew] last summer in Newport what was the object of this society and he replied "enjoyment." Then I looked about me. I saw beautiful women, lovely girls, great men, and I said to myself if the object of this society is enjoyment, it must be the highest, most exquisite enjoyment possible, an enjoyment that while being a delight for the time is also unconscious progression —as, listening to beautiful music, while your body is happy in the rhythm of sound your mind is progressing with the thought of the masters. I believe I have found for society a new method of translating this happy progression. As the musician uses his violin to tell of the highest thought, the singer the voice, I would use that greatest of all instruments, the human body, and its language would be movement.

The idea first came to me when a little girl, gazing at the reproduction of Botticelli's "Spring Time" which hung over our book case. It came to me what a wonderful movement there was in that picture, and how each figure through that movement told the story of its new life. And then as Mother played Mendelssohn's Spring Song, as if by the impulse of a gentle wind, the daisies in the grass would sway and the figures in the picture would move, and the Three Graces, arms twining together. . . .

(The earliest existing fragment of I. D.'s writings, this is from a sheet of notes, unpunctuated, for a lecture in New York, 1898 or 1899, before the first trip to Europe.)

✐ ✐ ✐ ✐

. . . If the dance is not to come to life again as an art, then far better that its name should rest in the dust of antiquity. . . . I am not at all interested in reforming anything. I am deeply interested in the question: Is the dance a sister art or no; and if so, how shall it be brought to life as an art? And I put this question quite apart from myself or of my dance, which may be nothing—or something—simply as a question which must be of interest to most people.

My dancing is to me an instinctive thing born with me. I danced when a little girl, because I had a passion for it, and since a very early age I have danced before the public. You call me a barefoot dancer. To me you might as well say a bare-headed or bare-handed dancer. I took off my clothes to dance because I felt the rhythm and freedom of my body better that way. In all ages when the dance was an art, the feet were left free as well as the rest of the body; also, whenever the dance has had an influence on the other arts—as in the beautiful bas-reliefs of dancing figures of the Greeks, and the lovely dancing figures of the Italians. Even when a painter or sculptor draws or models a dancing figure today, he generally portrays it with light draperies and without shoes.

If you would think of this a bit you would see that the conception of a dancing figure as being in light drapery and without shoes is not mine especially, but simply the ideal dancing figure as thought of by all artists of all times. Then you would cease to use the title "barefoot dancer," which I confess I detest; and you would see that in endeavoring to found a school for the renewing of the dance as an art, it is quite natural that the pupils should follow in their dress the hint given them by the Great Masters in portraying the dancing figure—insomuch as one takes as foundation principle that the dance is the body expressing itself in rhythmic movement.

I have danced before the public continuously since I was a little girl; in all these years, although certainly there has been much blame and discussion, there has been on the whole a general feeling of joyous acclaim and encouragement coming toward me from the public. It is this sort of joyous encouragement that has upborne me on my way, for I felt it was a sort of voice from the people that such a dance was wanted, *needed*. There seemed to be a longing for the rhythm of movement among them; and always along the route I have received thousands of letters from young girls. All these letters read in the same way: "All our lives we have felt a longing to dance, now we think you have found the right way; won't you teach us?"

Now I could not think that I could teach another what had been a gradual evolution of my own being and a work of all my life, but I felt I must give some response to all these questionings. And so the idea gradually came to me—ripening to a resolution which formed itself in my mind about ten years ago—to endeavor to found a school, whose object would be the finding of the true dancing. Not in any way a copy of my dance, but the study of the dance as an Art. I explained this purpose to my audiences in quite a simple way and they seemed to think it a good idea. Audiences in cities all over America, Germany, Austria, Hungary, France, wherever I told about it, replied, that is a good idea. I spoke always after I danced, and all those voices replied, we want that school. It was with the encouragement of these voices and the money earned from each representation that I at length founded the school in the year 1904. . . .

(From a handwritten draft of a letter to a Cologne newspaper editor, answering an article about an exhibition of the work of the school girls, December, 1906.)

DRAWING BY JOSÉ CLARÁ

DRAWING BY JOSÉ CLARÁ

That exact knowledge and feeling which the ancient Greeks possessed for human form and proportion is nowhere better realized than when one stands in the circular orchestra of the Theatre of Dionysus on the south side of the Acropolis. Putting one's self in the place of the actor, and facing the thirty thousand seats which rise in gradual sequence on the side of the hill, one feels how perfectly the soul of one man might control the spirit of the spectators so placed. . . .

✦ ✦ ✦ ✦

This figure is the best example I could give of an emotion taking entire possession of the body. The head is turned backward—but the movement of the head is not calculated; it is the result of the overwhelming feeling of Dionysiac ecstasy which is portrayed in the entire body. The chord from the lyre is still reverberating through all the members. If you had before you a dancer inspired with this feeling, it would be contagious. You would forget the dancer himself. You would only feel, as he feels, the chord of Dionysiac ecstasy.

(As an example of the notebook descriptions of works of art, mentioned in Essay XVII, this paragraph indicates the care with which the dancer studied out the figures in vase drawings, sculptures and paintings in the chief museums of Europe. Often there is hardly more than a reference to the subject of the art work, and a notation about its relation to the dance; at other times full descriptions like this.)

✦ ✦ ✦ ✦

I have noticed that when I introduce any innovation into my art, the music critics insult me in the same terms which they employ ten years later to honor my imitators.

✦ ✦ ✦ ✦

During the last ten years of my work I have steadily intended to found a school which should, if possible, restore dancing to its former eminence, to the eminence of an art. Many things have led me to believe that the art of dancing is in process of awakening. The contemplation of rhythmical movement is, and has ever been, a source of high pleasure to humanity. (It has been in every age a most important feature of religious ceremonies.) And the younger generation of artists and students are, at the present time, showing themselves eagerly desirous of some more perfect realization of the body in motion. The recognition accorded by the public to my efforts shows that I am not mistaken. Being convinced, therefore, that all that was needed was some one with a strong purpose who should come forward and induce others to assist and co-operate in the inauguration of a work which may lead to great developments in the future, I opened my new School of Dancing in December, 1904.

To rediscover the beautiful, rhythmical motions of the human body, to call back to life again that ideal movement which should be in harmony with the highest physical type, and to awaken once more an art which has slept for two thousand years—these are the serious aims of the school.

(Foreword for Grünewald School prospectus, "The Dance of the Future." 1906.)

↙ ↙ ↙ ↙

(The following three items are from the press files concerning the American tours of 1911 and 1915. They should be read, perhaps, as an afterpiece to *I See America Dancing*. The first paragraph is written in Isadora Duncan's hand at the end of a discarded bit of press agent's "copy," as a substitute for the polite, optimistic, and complimentary phrases of a well-meaning publicity writer. The second item is from an interview given in London in 1921, copyrighted under that date by the *Public Ledger* Company, and published in several American papers. Although in general I have discarded interviews as unreliable, this accords so closely with notes and letters of the time, that I have no doubt that it was either dictated by Miss Duncan, or actually written out in answer to a request for an interview. The third item is from Miss Duncan's curtain speech at Carnegie Hall, as reported in *The New York Evening World* of April 1, 1911. To these is added a fourth item, from a London press interview of 1921.)

I call my dance American rather than classic. By American I mean belonging to this country essentially. Just as the poetry of Walt Whitman springs from the womb of America, and the sculpture of George Grey Barnard, so my dance, having its origin in the very life sources of this country, is the dance which belongs to America. It will, I believe, be the foundation of a great school of dancing, joined with a new school of music, which will make this land joyous in the future. The school of the Ballet, having its birth in the epoch of Louis XIII, expresses in its movements and dress all the artificial culture of that time. It can never mean anything to the American people but a curious and wonderful gymnastic. The meaning of this dance in all its essentials is hidden from us. There will never be a school of the dance in America founded on the Ballet.

✧ ✧ ✧ ✧

America, when will you give me some response for what I might be to you? In 1898 you can read in the New York newspapers of my first struggles to give you my art. You will see some pictures of me then, a little girl seeking the first gesture and rhythm that would liberate the dance and teach the children and the youth to find the expression of their own free souls in movement. At that time your answer was to starve me almost to death and to cause me to fly from the country, coming to Europe on a cattle ship.

Only afterward, when all the great artists and publics of Europe had approved my work, you allowed my return in 1909 and gave me what is called in America a "great success," a success of a caprice of the moment, without heart or will power to understand what I had brought you and which led to a thousand or two copies and caricatures of my idea, spreading over the entire continent like a sickness.

Then after years of work I brought you my school in 1915 as a refuge from the war. You allowed these little pupils whom I had educated by the sacrifice of my entire fortune to be treated as outcasts, to suffer for lack of funds to keep them and finally to be turned out of the Century Theatre by the sheriff.

Finally, when forced to borrow the boat fare to return to France and friends, I left you my six eldest pupils, all the treasure of my sixteen years' effort and struggle; girls I had taught since they were six and eight years old, hoping to bring them up as true daughters of Walt Whitman, young goddesses of great, true movements, to teach hundreds of little children in the future.

You gave them also what you called a "great success"; that is, you allowed them to be exploited by managers from New York to San Francisco in what is called a theatrical tournee—one-night stands, and every day on the railway, until they were sent back to me this year, nervous and physical wrecks, victims of this cruel egotism of your managers and your sensation-loving public; those girls who might have been a source of light and beauty to all the children of America.

Do you wonder I am tired and discouraged? I know you will put up a monument to me fifty years after my death, but what good will that be? I will then be far away from the agony and struggle and unable to give you a great school and a great idea that you cannot understand or appreciate.

Still I send you my love and my hope.

In London when I danced they said my dances were taken from the Greek. It is not true. They are American. I am an American, born in California. My ancestors have lived in America for two hundred years. My dances are of the woods, the lakes, the rivers, the mountains and the prairies of my native land—aren't they? Some of the critics say my primitive art is monotonous, but if it has given a little joy to this great audience I am glad.

In dancing simply as dancing I am not interested. To me dancing must be the expression of life, not merely a series of gymnastic tricks or pretty movements. That is why I dislike the ordinary ballet dancing, which constrains people to adopt unnatural attitudes and cramps the free expression of their emotions.

To English people, with their fine athletic bodies, their wide, free movements, their natural grace of bearing, the ballet seems essentially unfitted. Perhaps that is why in the past there have been no great English ballet dancers.

English people have, I think, the wrong idea of beauty. To the majority it means something suave, softly pretty. To the artist beauty has a sterner meaning. Beauty to him is expression. Rodin's head of Balzac is ugly according to everyday standards, but artists know that because it is completely expressive it is the perfection of beauty. So with my new Slav dance, while I think it is the best thing I have done, many may think it ugly.

I want music, art, and drama to come together. The spoken word is essential; it is the heart and brains of the theatre. The other two are its lyric ecstasy. Then with these three and architecture and painting combined our theatres will become temples. All drama should have its foundation in religion, for without that it becomes ignoble.

What do I think of ballroom dancing? Chiefly I am amazed at the great restraint shown by the dancers, who, clasped in one another's arms, and moving to the most lascivious music, still continue to behave in the most orthodox manner.

⚜ ⚜ ⚜ ⚜

The dance is of the theatre at its most exalted moment. We must bring dancing again into the world for that purpose. With that ideal in mind I have again and again given up my personal career, as I did in 1905 when I adopted forty children to give them this art. It would have been simpler, easier, to go my own way prosperously. But I knew that some day the drama of the future would utilize dance as nobly as did that of the Greeks. Or that out of the dance the new drama might grow. But the world is impatient in these modern times. It is not willing to wait; it wants "results." It could not wait for a new thing to grow up naturally and beautifully. It begrudged the means, it tempted the individual dancers to go out to win personal successes in the market places. It has destroyed each successive school that I have founded.

But the dance will return as I have visioned it. Mankind will not always expect those with vision to put a seed in the ground and bring it to flowering in a single night. Even now I am planning again for my long cherished school. In Moscow a school I have started promises perhaps to bring the ideal to fruition—not this year or next, but when children have grown up with nature, with beauty, with the thought of the dance in music and in tragedy.

(Added to earlier articles, to close an essay for *Theatre Arts Monthly*, 1927.)

❧   ❧   ❧   ❧

I spent long days and nights in the studio seeking that dance which might be the divine expression of the human spirit through the medium of the body's movement. For hours I would stand quite still, my two hands folded between my breasts, covering the solar plexus. . . . I was seeking and finally discovered the central spring of all movement, the crater of motor power, the unity from which all diversities of movement are born, the mirror of vision for the creation of the dance. It was from this discovery that was born the theory on which I founded my school. The ballet school taught the pupils that this spring was found in the center of the back at the base of the spine. From this axis, says the ballet master, arms, legs and trunk must move freely, giving the result of an articulated puppet. This method produces an artificial mechanical movement not worthy of the soul.

I on the contrary sought the source of spiritual expression, from which would flow into the channels of the body, filling it with vibrating light, the centrifugal force reflecting the spirit's vision. After many months, when I had learned to concentrate all my force in this one center, I found that thereafter when I listened to music the rays and vibrations of the music streamed to this one fount of light within me, where they reflected themselves in Spiritual Vision, not the mirror of the brain but of the soul; and from this vision I could express them in Dance. . . .

The peculiar environment of my childhood and youth had developed this power in me to a very great degree, and in different epochs of my life I have been enabled to shut out all outside influences and to live in this force alone. . . .

I also then dreamed of finding a first movement from which would be born a series of movements without my volition, but as the unconscious re-action of the primary movement. I had developed this movement in a series of different variations on several themes, such as the first movement of fear, followed by the natural re-actions born of the primary emotion, or Sorrow, from which would flow a dance of lamentation, or a love movement from the unfolding of which like the petals of a flower the dancer would stream as a perfume. . . .

(This and the following two excerpts are from *My Life*.)

4

I felt such sympathy with Walter Damrosch that it seemed to me when I stood in the center of the stage to dance, I was connected by every nerve in my body with the orchestra and with the great conductor.

How can I describe the joy of dancing with this orchestra? It is there before me—Walter Damrosch raises his baton—I watch it, and, at the first stroke there surges within me the combined symphonic chord of all the instruments in one. The mighty reverberation rushes over me and I become the medium to condense in unified expression the joy of Brünnhilde awakened by Siegfried, or the soul of Isolde seeking in Death her realization. Voluminous, vast, swelling like sails in the wind, the movements of my dance carry me onward—onward and upward; and I feel the presence of a mighty power within me which listens to the music and then reaches out through all my body, trying to find an outlet for this listening. Sometimes this power grew furious, sometimes it raged and shook me until my heart nearly burst from its passion, and I thought my last moments on earth had surely arrived. At other times it brooded heavily, and I would suddenly feel such anguish that, through my arms stretched to the Heavens, I implored help from where no help came. Often I thought to myself, what a mistake to call me a dancer—I am the magnetic center to convey the emotional expression of the Orchestra. From my soul sprang fiery rays to connect me with my trembling vibrating Orchestra.

There was a flutist who played so divinely the solo of the Happy Spirits in *Orpheus* that I often found myself immobile on the stage, with the tears flowing from my eyes, just from the ecstasy of listening to him, and the singing of the violins and the whole orchestra soaring upwards, inspired by the wonderful conductor.

There was a marvelous sympathy between Damrosch and me, and to each one of his gestures I instantly felt the answering vibration. As he augmented the crescendo in volume, so the life in me mounted and overflowed in gesture—for each musical phrase translated into a musical movement, my whole being vibrated in harmony with his.

PHOTOGRAPH BY STEICHEN

PHOTOGRAPH BY STEICHEN

Man must speak, then sing, then dance. But the speaking is the brain, the thinking man. The singing is the emotion. The dancing is the Dionysian ecstasy which carries away all.

✓ ✓ ✓ ✓

I have read in your issue of September 27th an article in which it is stated that I "will appear soon in some antique Greek dances," and "with sumptuous costumes." It would be impossible to give a description of my art more completely false.

Certainly, like every artist of our time, I have been inspired by Greek art, since it is the foundation of all our Western culture. Certainly it is true that in a period of sixteen years I have gone eight times to Greece, and that I remained there each time as long as my economic circumstances permitted—for to live in Greece is to know the very source of Beauty, the inspiration of my art. But that is far from saying that I wish to revive the ancient dances.

To revive the antique dances would be a task as impossible as it would be useless. The dance, to be an art for us, must be born out of ourselves, out of the emotions and the life of our times, just as the old dances were born of the life and the emotions of the ancient Greeks. To be sure, in my youth I spent long hours of enthusiastic admiration before the Parthenon, before the friezes, the frescos, the vases, the Tanagra figures.

But that was not as a step toward *copying* either the attitudes or the excellencies of those masterpieces. On the contrary, I studied them so long in order to steep myself in the spirit underlying them, in order to discover the secret of the ecstasy in them, putting myself into touch with the feelings that their gestures symbolized. Thus, in taking my soul back to the mystic sources of their rapture, I have, on my own part, found again the secret of Beauty that resides in that Holy of

Holies. Out of that has come my dancing, neither Greek nor antique, but the spontaneous expression of my soul lifted up by beauty.

For me Dionysus is not dead. He is the eternal God, all-powerful, who under many names and in many forms inspires every creative artist: Krishna, Osiris, Dionysus—and let us remember that Nietzsche signed his last message *"Dionysus Crucified."*

As to the second part of your article, which speaks of the sumptuousness of my costumes, I have never worn antique costumes or rich ones, because the dance is for me the expression of the body reflecting the soul in ecstasy.

Neither by gestures and attitudes nor by costumes and cunning draperies, but only in terms of the human body can the dance convey its message to humanity: the double message of Apollo and Dionysus—to the divine music of Bach, Beethoven, Schubert, Wagner, the great mystics and prophets of our era.

(From a letter published in the *Progrès d'Athènes,* in 1920. Here translated from the French—as are all of the next six items.)

✦ ✦ ✦ ✦

It is possible to dance in two ways:

One can throw oneself into the spirit of the dance, and dance the thing itself: *Dionysus.*

Or one can *contemplate* the spirit of the dance—and dance as one who relates a story: *Apollo.*

✦ ✦ ✦ ✦

All promise for the future I see in a great school where children will learn to dance, to sing, to live for the Wisdom and the Beauty of the world.

Rodin has written: "When Nature is understood, then Progress has begun."

That the child should understand Nature, it must dance according to Nature's rhythm. The great event of this era will be the awakening of the Dance as a noble art, sister to Music. The dance for two thousand years has been an art imprisoned. All my life I have been trying to break its chains, to open the gates and give it back its freedom. Once liberated, the dance will be the great inspirational force among the arts: sculpture, painting, architecture will find new wings, and tragedy will live again.

When the dance died tragedy died, for the dance is the Dionysian spirit in tragedy, and without the dance tragedy has lost its reason for being.

Before I danced, all dancers were imprisoned in tight clothes, repeating year after year some mechanical gestures; since I began thousands of people have begun dancing, in all the countries of the world, clothed only in light tunics, and knowing for the first time the free rhythm of the human body, and its accordance with the harmonious movements of Nature; thousands are seeking spontaneous movement, and the relationship of this to great music. Schools have been established, in accordance with my ideas, in every country, from Finland to South America. Unfortunately these schools have adopted the letter of my teaching but not its spirit.

They copy the movements—but ignore the secret of the inner impulse.

(From a letter to a French Government official, appealing for a school.)

To dance is to live. What I want is a *school of life,* for man's greatest riches are in his soul, in his imagination. There may be a life after this one, but I know not what we shall have there. This is what I do know: our riches here on earth are in our will, our inner life.

What is the first law for all art? What answer would a great sculptor or a great painter make? I think simply this: "Look at Nature, study Nature, understand Nature—and then try to express Nature."

The dance is an art like these others, and it also must find its beginning in this great first principle: *Study Nature*.

You answer, "How can a dancer study first in the realm of Nature, when the dance consists of hundreds of steps, and these steps are set down in the books on the art of the dance, and when there are all the rules and teachings of the ballet masters? If you wish to be dancers you must find a teacher of the dance."

And I would reply: "The dance does not consist of all that: the dance is the movements of the human body in harmony with the movements of the earth; and if it does not accord with those movements, it is false."

That is the first law for the study of the dance: study the movements of Nature.

✓ ✓ ✓ ✓

The dance is not a diversion but a religion, an expression of life. I teach that to the young children in my school; I know nothing about those who make a mere amusement of the dance. Life is the root and art is the flower.

How do these things concern me? One does not ask Rodin to watch the young girls of the world playing at sculpture. Why should I watch them dance?

(From an interview given to a French newspaper, in French, in answer to a question about her attitude toward the fashionable dances.)

✓ ✓ ✓ ✓

True art comes from within and has no need for exterior decorations. In my school we have neither rich costumes nor ornaments, but only the beauty that rises out of the soul with the coming of inspiration, and out of the body which is its symbol.

If my art has been able to teach anything, I hope it is that beauty can be found in the play of children and in the artlessness of their open hands.

You have seen them today, forming a circle or crossing the stage—surely they are more lovely than any necklace of pearls! These are my jewels, and I do not desire any others.

Give beauty, give freedom, give health to the children; give art to the people who ask for it. Great music ought not to serve only for the pleasure of those who are specially privileged; it should be given free to the masses. Art and music are as necessary to the people as the air or bread, because art is the spiritual bread of mankind.

✦ ✦ ✦ ✦

I believe in each life is a spiritual line, an upward curve. And all that adheres to or strengthens this line is our real life; the rest is but as chaff falling from one's progress. Such a spiritual line is my Art.

✦ ✦ ✦ ✦

My life has known but two motives—Love and Art. And often Love destroyed Art—and often the imperious call of Art put a tragic end to Love—for these two have known no accord but constant battle.

✦ ✦ ✦ ✦

Memory, Memory—what is Memory?

A cracked tankard from which the wine has all leaked out, leaving it dry and to quench no thirst.

When I try to remember events that were so marvelous, so vibrant—like an apple orchard bursting with ripe apples—and when I put this in these words, a medium I don't understand, they seem like dead leaves, dry, parched, no juice or interest left—but that is because I am not a writer. When I dance it is different.

On the temple-crownèd summit
    Breaks again the rising day,
Streaming with its dawning brightness
    Down the waters of the bay!

See, the centuried mist is breaking!
    Lo, the free Hellenic shore!
Marathon—Plataea tells us
    Greece is living Greece once more.

(Two verses from "INTAGLIO: Lines on a Beautiful Greek Antique," by Joseph Charles Duncan, father of Isadora. From "Outcroppings," a selection of California verse edited by Bret Harte.)

PHOTOGRAPH BY STEICHEN

EDITOR'S NOTES

1. PAGE 47. *I See America Dancing*. Because there are several different versions, I have gone back to the original handwritten ms. It is in two parts, as indicated here by the break after the paragraph ending "the America of Abraham Lincoln." There is latitude for variant readings, but Isadora Duncan did not write "the kindness and purity of our statesmen," as in the other published versions. One transcriber or editor also changed "worthy of the name of Democracy" to "worthy of the name of the *greatest* Democracy" —prettily localizing the sentiment for home consumption. First published in the New York *Herald-Tribune,* October 2, 1927. Re-printed in *My Life,* and copyrighted, 1927, by Boni & Liveright, Inc.

2. PAGE 51. *The Philosopher's Stone of Dancing*. Probably first written as a program note, this has been widely published. Several mss. also exist, with wide variations. There are two different English versions, but the one I have discarded seems quite obviously a re-translation back into English from a French translation. One version is dated 1920, but parts may have been written very much earlier.

3. PAGE 54. *The Dance of the Future*. Delivered as a lecture in Berlin, 1903. Published in Leipzig by Eugen Diederichs in that year. First published in America under the title "The Dance," in a souvenir program. There copyrighted, 1909, by Charles Douville Coburn, Miss Duncan's American representative.

4. PAGE 64. *The Parthenon*. A fragment handwritten in a notebook of the first Athens period—in the same book that has the rules for conduct at Kopanos (see *My Life,* pages 126-7).

5. PAGE 66. *The Dancer and Nature*. This essay was originally written as a dialogue between two people floating "in a little bark becalmed" off the shores of Greece; but in a less sentimental moment I. D. or another blue-pencilled all but the lines carrying the main thought, without adding transitional sentences between the remaining fragments— which explains a certain jerkiness. The one fairly complete ms., moreover, is badly typed and probably lacks several pages. Still it has seemed worth while to reconstruct the essay, as a reflection of the dancer's thoughts in those days when she was deeply in love with Greek art and German philosophy, and lecturing to Berlin women about the free woman's body. Necessarily this is the most edited and least finished of all the essays— with even the expressive capital letters left just as they were.

6. PAGE 71. *What Dancing Should Be*. Another incomplete ms., with one page missing, and evidently typed by a German secretary little acquainted with English. From marginal notations I judge the essay to have been written in Berlin in 1905 or 1906. Where the page is missing I have set in, as indicated, a fragment which seems to carry on the thought—though it may be a later work and now exists in French only.

7. PAGE 74. *A Child Dancing*. Dated "Noordwijk aan Zee, 22nd August, 1906." First published, in German translation, in the *Frankfurter Zeitung* four days later. I have restored the original first paragraph, in place of a version added in 1925 or 1926.

8. PAGE 77. *Movement Is Life*. The first part is from a typed ms. The balance exists in two versions each with parts not in the other, and with many variations in wording. Probably first published in English in 1909, in a New York recital program.

9. PAGE 80. *Beauty and Exercise*. I have suspected that this only discovered English version is a translation, none too carefully worded; but in the absence of decisive evidence I have admitted it here practically without change. Probably first appeared in French in 1914.

10. PAGE 84. *The Dance in Relation to Tragedy*. An older article, rewritten in 1927 for *Theatre Arts Monthly*.

11. PAGE 86. *The Greek Theatre*. Probably first printed in *Dionysion*, published by "the Committee for the Furtherance of Isadora Duncan's work in America," New York, 1915. Copyright by Isadora Duncan, 1915.

12. PAGE 88. *Education and the Dance*. An older article or program note, made over in 1927, and added to two earlier works to complete an article for *Theatre Arts Monthly*.

13. PAGE 90. *Terpsichore*. The mss. and published versions vary greatly. To complete the English text I have had to translate several paragraphs from the French (see next note). One version is dated 1909.

14. PAGE 92. *The Dance of the Greeks*. This and the following three essays, 14 to 17, and also 22, are translations into English from French mss., program notes, etc., made since Isadora Duncan's death. Some she undoubtedly wrote in French (the handwritten mss. exist), but others are patently French translations from English texts now missing. Some of the originals will perhaps be found again—the dancer's papers were scattered literally to the ends of the earth, from California to Russia; but it is probable that no one will ever know whether others were originally written in French or English. Those readers who may care to go back to the available French texts will find a considerable collection in a pamphlet entitled *La Danse, par Isadora Duncan,* printed for the dancer by Raymond Duncan in Paris, 1927; and about the same amount of material, with important additions and equally important omissions, in *Ecrits sur la Danse, par Isadora Duncan,* Paris, Editions du Grenier [1928]. Each of these collections contains about one-third of the writings on the art of the dance as they appear in the present volume.

18. PAGE 105. *Richard Wagner*. Written in French in the form of a letter to *La Herse,* and published there in 1921.

19. PAGE 107. A letter to the group of six pupils who were dancing in America. 1918 or 1919.

21. PAGE 116. *Reflections, after Moscow.* Written in the form of a letter, in French, and here translated from a ms. draft.

22. PAGE 121. *Dancing in Relation to Religion and Love.* One of the last essays, written in 1927 for *Theatre Arts Monthly*. Reprinted without change, except for two paragraphs dropped because taken from *The Dance of the Future.*

Art

792.8092 DUNCAN
Duncan, Isadora,
1877-1927.
The art of the dance.